Endorsements

Believe and Receive Your Miracle, Today is a book born out of a heart for God—His Glory, His Presence, His Love, and His Power to heal and set free all who are in need of a miracle. If you're hurting, suffering, or need to be delivered from something, this book is a reality.

There is always a price to pay for writing a book like this. It's born out of life's many trials and testing. Mary Ellen Gordon went through many of these to reach the point of freedom to be able to point the way, through Scripture, to those who are searching for answers.

In a clear and concise way, she presents a path through the Word that makes healing possible. The testimonies and points to meditate upon, will give you a fresh vision of the love that Jesus has for you. Pastor Gordon writes with a humble and open spirit that will challenge your belief that Jesus is the real Healer.

Once you read this, your hunger to chase after the ONE who loves you most will increase into a new relationship. After that—all things are possible. Yes, even miracles!

Pastor Don Schiemant/Director
Healing Rooms of Buffalo Niagara

The book, *Believe and Receive Your Miracle, Today* will inspire and train you in God's approach to receiving healing and miracles. As Mary Ellen Gordon explains, there are a number of steps to receiving divine healing and in releasing miracles as Jesus intended. You do need to give attention to the various parts of the healing process. Pastor Gordon has listed these parts and as you read and meditate on this book, it will cause you to review these necessary steps and ask, "Lord, am I taking this step so that my miracle can be released?" Truly, this book can be the key to releasing the miracle you have been seeking.

Dr. Mark Virkler
Communion With God Ministries
Author of "4 Keys to Hearing God's Voice"
President of Christian Leadership University

As every child of God seeks the will and the life-changing power of God upon their life, we learn that His Word is the light and the quickening unto our way. You will find that *Believe and Receive Your Miracle, Today* is an inspiring declaration of the promises of our Lord for His miracle touch into all circumstances.

Pastor Simeon Strauser
Chairman, Full Gospel Assemblies International
Parksburg, Pennsylvania USA

Believe and Receive Your Miracle, Today

Mary Ellen Gordon

Gotham Books

30 N Gould St.
Ste. 20820, Sheridan, WY 82801
https://gothambooksinc.com/

Phone: 1 (307) 464-7800

© 2025 *Mary Ellen Gordon*. All rights reserved.

No part of this book may be reproduced, stored in a retrieval system, or transmitted by any means without the written permission of the author.

Published by Gotham Books (April 12, 2025)

ISBN: 979-8-3482-6915-9 (P)
ISBN: 979-8-3482-6916-6 (E)

Because of the dynamic nature of the Internet, any web addresses or links contained in this book may have changed since publication and may no longer be valid.

The views expressed in this work are solely those of the author and do not necessarily reflect the views of the publisher, and the publisher hereby disclaims any responsibility for them.

Dedication

I would like to dedicate this writing to my Lord, Jesus Christ, who spoke in an inner audible voice and gave me the idea in the first place. For His unconditional love and faithfulness in making what once seemed impossible, now a miraculous reality. To Him be all the glory!

Special thanks to Pastor Don Schiemant, for his support and encouragement, as I began to take steps of faith to fulfill the vision God has given for Healing Deliverance Ministry.

To those whose input and support have also made the publishing of this book possible, along with all of our faithful ministry prayer partners who have prayed and supported this project and *Waves of Glory Miracle Ministries* in so many ways since its inception.

Finally, to you, the reader, whom I believe is in need of a miracle. May you receive and act upon God-given revelations from the Holy Spirit that will bring healing and wholeness to your life so that you can walk in your full inheritance in Christ, which was purchased for you on Calvary's cross. Also, that this book would equip you to then minister to others 'the truth' so that they too can receive their miracle!

Contents

Preface 1

Prologue 2

Chapter 1 Lord, I Need a Miracle 5

Chapter 2 Is God Still Doing Miracles Today? 13

Chapter 3 Believing For Your Miracle 22

Chapter 4 Receiving Your Miracle 40

Chapter 5 Keeping Your Miracle 55

Chapter 6 Your Miracle Is In Your Mouth 68

Chapter 7 Hindrances to Your Miracle 75

Chapter 8 The Miracle of Deliverance 82

Chapter 9 The Miracle of Inner Healing 91

Chapter 10 The Greatest Miracle of All 105

Epilogue 110

Declare Your Miracle 114

Prayers that Avail Much 122

Recommended Reading for Further Study 127

Bibliography 129

About the Author 130

Preface

Casting all your care upon him;
for He careth for you.

1 Peter 5:7

You may be weighed down with the cares of this world, feeling overwhelmed and without hope—not knowing where to turn or if there really is help for you.

It is out of a heart of *great compassion* that the Lord has commissioned this writing. He knows your every need, and He wants to meet your need passionately *today*. Come and find comfort *in the truth* from God's Word, which will *set you free*. Let the cry of your heart find rest for your soul, knowing that His desire to give of Himself to you is far greater than your desire to receive your miracle from Him.

Let *divine revelation*, which we will discuss, be *imprinted deeply* upon your heart as you *ponder the truth.* Don't be quick to go from one thought to another, but rather stay with what the Lord reveals to you—until faith arises and a settled peace pervades your innermost being.

Let my cry come near before thee, O Lord;
Give me understanding according to thy word.

Psalms 119:169

Prologue

"Let the Truth Be Told! Shout It from the Rooftops!"

> What I tell you in darkness,
> that speak ye in light; and what ye hear in the ear,
> that preach ye upon the housetops.
>
> Matthew 10:27

The fact that you are holding this book in your hand would indicate that you probably need a miracle or know someone who does. You may be thinking, *What could this person possibly have to say that's any different from other writers? Can I really experience a miracle? Can I really be healed and delivered? Can I find the peace I so desperately need from the struggles of life, which seem so overwhelming at times?* I've got good news for you. Yes, indeed you can!

My purpose in writing this book is to share with you as simplistically as possible, *the truth* that you must know through *divine revelations* from the Word of God. You will find answers to questions you may have, which will help you receive the miracle that you need, and you will learn how to live life in the *supernatural*, where miracles happen every day!

Know that this book is not intended to be read as a *quick read-through*. Rather, it will require that you *stop* and *meditate* upon the text and scriptures from time to time with *frequent review*, which will increase your faith for "faith comes by hearing, and hearing by the Word of God" (Romans 10:17).

We need to know *the truth* through God-given revelations. These revelations are necessary in order to fully comprehend all that you must know and do to live a *lifestyle* of miracles. Miracles should be the *norm*—not just the occasional supernatural happening for a few. Whether or not you have some knowledge of God's Word, you must receive the revelation or *illumination* of that Word, which brings *enlightenment* through the presence and power of the Holy Spirit.

Bruce Wilkinson, in his book *The Prayer of Jabez* has written, "Life change takes place when you change *how you think*. Truth is wasted in our lives, if we don't *'put it to work'* to accomplish what God intends."

If ye continue in my word... ye shall know the truth,
and the truth shall make you free.

John 8:31-32

Wilkinson goes on to say, "Yet, most of us are only beginners at 'experiencing' God's blessings, because we haven't let *the truth* set us free, by changing what we *think and do*."

What do we mean by divine revelation? Revelation is the knowledge of God's Word which is *suddenly revealed* to your spirit by the Holy Spirit without prior knowledge. Today, God is restoring *Biblical Truth* through new revelations, which have not always been known or taught throughout the history of the church. Tragically, *the truth* has been replaced with much that is often untrue. (3 John 2) says that God wants each of us to prosper in all things and be blessed with divine health and freedom from every form of bondage or loss.

Whatever you need, be it financial, relational, or a need for healing in your body, mind, or emotions—the fact is that many are receiving and have received their miracle. So why should you be any different? We know from Scripture that God is no *respecter of persons* (Acts 10:34). This means what He has done for others, *He will do for you!*

But you may be thinking... *How can this be? I've tried everything I know to do!* Just the fact that you need a miracle indicates that there remain perhaps *key truths* that you must come to understand and embrace by revelation from God's Word, and when you do, you can and will experience your miracle.

Let me take you step by step through a few *key revelations* that can make all the difference. Then together, we will believe for your miracle!

My people are destroyed for lack of knowledge: because thou hast rejected knowledge, I will also reject thee...

Hosea 4:6

The fact is that God longs to set you free from everything that is holding you *hostage*—sickness and disease, tormenting thoughts and emotional wounds from the past, and impossible circumstances that threaten to destroy everything you hold dear. Whatever you need, let's trust God together. Take my hand and know you are not alone.

God has a miracle for you *today!*

Blessed is the man that trusteth in the Lord,
and whose hope the Lord is.

Jeremiah 17:7

Chapter 1

Lord, I Need a Miracle

Delight thyself (enjoy serving) also in the Lord;
And He shall give thee the desires of thine heart.
Commit thy way unto the Lord;
Trust also in Him, and He shall bring it to pass.

Psalms 37:4-5

I am so delighted that you have chosen to join me as we explore the truth together. I assure you that you will not be disappointed. God has spoken clearly in His Word all that you need to know and do to experience your miracle today.

However, as we begin, it is important that we settle in our hearts that the Word of God is indeed *the truth*. We need to come to God's Word afresh, with open hearts, so that the Holy Spirit can teach us with the mind of Christ. Again, this is so important! So as we do...

Let's Pray Together, Out Loud!

Lord Jesus, I come into Your presence with eyes focused on You alone. Help me to hear, understand, and receive revelation from Your Holy Spirit. Teach me. Open the eyes of my heart to Your Spirit. I renounce anything that would hinder me from receiving all that You have for me. In Your precious name, I pray. Amen.

If ye continue in my word...
ye shall know the truth,
and the truth shall make you free.

John 8:31-32

Let's begin once again by taking a closer look at the above scripture. The word to *know* means to *experience* for yourself. Therefore, if we are to fully *know the truth*, we must experience the truth. That is to say, when you have experienced your miracle, then you will know *the truth*, and that truth will totally have set you free. This is the will of God for you!

Stop! Meditate here for a moment on this important truth!

Remember, as we continue, there will be times when you will need *to ponder* or give *thorough consideration* to the truth being discussed—letting its meaning deeply penetrate every fiber of your being.

To fully know the truth we must experience the truth!

It is important that you know beyond a shadow of a doubt that it is God's will that you understand and *experience the truth*, because of His great love for you. Take some time here to *meditate* and even *memorize* the following scriptures, which will increase your faith and help you to *believe* for your miracle.

As we proceed, we must always stand firm against anything that seems to contradict God's Word, even when circumstances, our five senses, symptoms of illness, and our thoughts and *sound reasoning* seem to indicate otherwise.

Meditate upon these things; give thyself wholly to them; that thy profiting may appear to all.

1 Timothy 4:15

I can do all things through Christ who strengthens me.

Philippians 4:13

Take time to meditate and ponder the truth thoroughly!

Beloved, I wish above all things that thou mayest prosper and be in health, even as thy soul prospereth. For I rejoiced greatly, when the brethren came and testified of the truth that is in thee, even as thou walkest in the truth. I have no greater joy than to hear that my children walk in truth.

3 John 2-4

If any of you lack wisdom, let him ask of God, that giveth to all men liberally, and upbraideth not, (without reproach) and it shall be given him. But let him ask in faith, nothing wavering: for he that wavereth is like a wave of the sea driven with the wind and tossed. For let not that man think that he shall receive anything of the Lord.

James 1:5-7

If ye abide in me, (live in me and believe) and my words abide in you, ye shall ask what ye will, and it shall be done unto you.

John 15:7

The Prayer of Agreement

Again I say unto you, "That if two of you shall agree on earth as touching anything that they shall ask, it shall be done for them of my Father which is in heaven."

Matthew 18:19

Keeping these scriptures in mind, I now set my faith with yours today, to believe with you for your miracle. Let's make the following confession together out loud.

Confession of Faith

Dear Lord Jesus, I want to know *the truth* from Your Word so that I can experience my miracle. I need to know beyond a shadow of a doubt that what You have said, You will do. I declare, as I continue to learn more, that I have the faith to believe for my miracle. In Your name, I pray. Amen.

What God has done for others He will do for you!

Stop! Take extra time, and meditate here on the above scriptures!

You may be still thinking at this point, *But how can you be so sure? Please hear me!*

The Faithfulness of God

As previously stated, our God shows *no partiality* (Acts 10:34). What He has done for me and many others, He will also do for you. Yes, I have and I am experiencing divine healing and health in my physical body, my mind, and my emotions on a continuing basis, as I act upon *the truth* of God's Word. I have seen God's faithfulness to provide all of my needs after much suffering and loss. God has truly restored much of what the enemy has stolen so that I can now cooperate with Him to fulfill my divine destiny. You can too!

The Power of the Testimony

Lives change when we share our testimony with others!

Know that as we continue, testimonies of various healings and miracles will be shared, which will build your faith so that you too can *believe and receive* your miracle! You will read real-life stories of people just like yourself. So let's now consider the following *miracle testimony* as we read on together. It is a wonderful example of how, after hearing *the truth* from the Word of God, a long-awaited miracle was manifested.

And they overcame him by the blood of the Lamb, and by the word of their testimony.

Revelation 12:11

Severe Back Pain Healed

Many today suffer with varying degrees of pain in various parts of the body. I have witnessed miracles of healing where lives have been restored, often after years of suffering with many forms of pain. Many suffer with debilitating back pain, though doctors have tried everything they know—leaving their patients with little hope. Nevertheless, as we look to God, our Healer and Deliverer, miracles are still happening every day!

Mark visited one of our healing prayer meetings with severe lower back pain, which for many years had kept him unable to hold a job. Mark's faith to believe for his miracle was strengthened after hearing a message from the Word of God on healing and divine health. After being anointed, I prayed the *prayer of faith* for a miracle, and he felt the power of God touch him. After checking his back, he discovered that all the pain was gone. He could now move freely and do what he could not do before with no pain, whatsoever. "And the prayer of faith shall save the sick, and the Lord shall raise him up" (James 5:15). Know that many others have been healed of painful symptoms as well, and so can you!

Surely he (Jesus) hath borne our griefs (diseases), and carried our sorrows; (pains).

Isaiah 53:4

An Important Reminder

As we continue, let me say once again that the importance of *key revelations* will be emphasized throughout this writing. As previously stated, we must grasp *the truth* through God-given revelations. Receiving and understanding these revelations in our spirit by the Holy Spirit are absolutely necessary in order to fully comprehend all that you must know and do to receive your miracle. Know that everything we receive from God requires a revelation that brings illumination. This enables us to release our faith and partake of all that God has provided for us through His atoning sacrifice on the cross of Calvary.

Therefore, do take the time to thoroughly *meditate* on each of the *ten key revelations* we will be discussing. We must have more than a *head-knowledge* of these truths contained in the Word of God. We must *know that we know* that God has already made every provision for us so that we can experience a life of abundant miracles. (John 10:10).

First Revelation: Revelation of the Truth

I need to know *the truth* through divine revelation from the Word of God, which will build my faith so I too can experience my miracle!

Everything we receive from God requires a revelation!

Chapter Review!

1. Knowing and experiencing the truth by revelation is key to receiving my miracle.
2. If I doubt God's Word, I should not expect to receive anything from Him.
3. God is no respecter of persons. What He has done for others, He will do for me.

And ye shall seek me, and find me, when ye shall search for me with all your heart.

Jeremiah 29:13

Stop! Continue to meditate on the above chapter before going on to the next!

Now, let's continue to discuss these truths through the revelations God has given us that you must *embrace by faith*. Then, as you do your part, I will help you take the needed steps in order to receive your miracle.

In the following chapter, we will discuss an important question that many ask today. Settling this question in your heart and mind *once and for all* is so important, if you are to have the faith you need to experience your miracle.

Chapter 2

Is God Still Doing Miracles Today?

*Jesus Christ the same yesterday,
and today, and forever.*

Hebrews 13:8

The *good news* is that if you need a touch from God, Jesus wants to touch every circumstance of your life and bring healing and deliverance to you *today*! Be assured, God is still restoring lives, as He did over 2,000 years ago. The Word of God is filled with many scriptures confirming God's will. Know that He has already made every provision for you. Again, God's desire is that you "be in health and prosper" in every area of your life (3 John 2). Here are some more of my favorite scriptures for meditation.

Jesus wants to touch you, heal you and deliver you today!

Incline thine ear unto my sayings,
Let them not depart from thine eyes;
Keep them in the midst of thine heart,
For they are life unto those who find them,
And health to all their flesh.

Proverbs 4:21–22

If thou wilt diligently hearken to the voice of the Lord thy God, I wilt put none of these diseases upon thee for I am the Lord that healeth thee.

Exodus 15:26

I will take sickness away from the midst of thee.

Exodus 23:25

He healeth the broken in heart, And bindeth up their wounds.

Psalms 147:3

I will restore health unto thee, And I will heal thee of thy wounds.

Jeremiah 30:17

I have seen the affliction of my people,....and I have heard their groaning, and am come down to deliver them.

Acts 7:34

And Jesus went about all the cities and villages, teaching in their synagogues, and preaching the gospel of the kingdom, and healing every sickness and every disease among the people.

Matthew 9:35

How God anointed Jesus of Nazareth with the Holy Ghost and with power; who went about doing good, and healing all who were oppressed of the devil; for God was with him.

Acts 10:38

Stop! Let the understanding of each scripture deeply penetrate your spirit. Know that God is the great I Am who is always present to perform miracles today!

Divine Health and Every Provision

A number of years ago, as I earnestly sought to fulfill my destiny, I began to study the *Healing Deliverance Ministry*. My heart is full of compassion for you, and I have a passion to see you *saved, healed, and set free* today. You are precious to God, and He wants to bless you abundantly.

I have learned truths from God's Word, which I have applied to my own life. Knowing that divine health and wholeness are mine through *Christ's sufferings* on the cross of Calvary, I no longer accept harmful circumstances or any diagnosis, symptoms of illness, or torment and oppression of any kind, and I *resist* them with the *authority* God has given me and every believer in Christ (Titus 2:15).

God is raising up healing deliverance ministries to bring forth the truth as never before!

For too long, we have accepted painful circumstances and physical, mental, and emotional problems with little or no resistance—not knowing or having been taught that we can walk free from much suffering. We have an adversary! Make no mistake about it. Satan wants to "steal, kill, and destroy" everything in your life (John 10:10).

John Avanzini has written in his book *Stolen Property Returned*, "The thief I speak of (Satan) is a deceptive, calculating plunderer, who has *moved freely* in and out of our lives. This ruthless destroyer has defrauded *or robbed every individual* on the face of this planet. He robs them of their money, relationships, peace of mind, health, as well as physical possessions."

Committed To Stand

Sickness, suffering, or loss of any kind are *no longer an option*, and I will continue to stand and resist any attempt of the enemy to take what is mine, while teaching others to do the same. Understand, I have not always had this strong conviction. However, I have found, along with many others, that when applying *the truth* to our individual lives, healing and deliverance are manifested, and that which has been destroyed is restored. Know that it is my prayer that you too will experience the same and find *freedom* and *release* in your life. (John 3:21) says, "But he that doeth truth cometh to the light, that his deeds may be made manifest, that they are wrought in God."

There are many *testimonies* of miracles and healings that have occurred and continue to occur here and throughout the world. Jesus is still caring for His precious people, and He will continue to do so today and in the future.

Our Heavenly Father is grieved to see the suffering all around us. This is the reason why He sent His son Jesus to earth, to be a sacrifice for sin and all suffering so that we could walk in divine health and be free from every form of bondage.

Today, Jesus is raising up many healing deliverance ministries, which are called to bring forth this truth. As founder of *Waves of Glory Miracle Ministries*, I am committed to this *mandate*.

(You can visit our website for further information at *www.wavesofglorymiracleministry.wordpress.com*)

Practicing the Truth

In 2011, while I had closed myself away to wait upon the Lord, seeking to hear His voice and receive direction for further ministry, God spoke in an *inner audible voice*. "Let the truth be told! Shout it from the rooftops!" At that time, He commissioned the writing of this book, which I believe He will use to set you free and many others for His glory.

Jesus has done all that He is going to do. "It's finished!"

Nevertheless, many continue to ask, "If all this is true, then why are so many suffering still today?" It is very important that we understand the answer to this question. The fact is that many have yet to take hold of *the truth* of what Jesus really accomplished at the whipping post and on the cross of Calvary. Jesus purchased not only our full redemption, which included *payment for sin*, but He also made provision for *divine health* and *deliverance* from all that seeks to bring harm and hold us captive. Again, we must embrace these revelatory truths if we are to walk in our full inheritance in Christ.

Also, there are *conditions* that, when understood and acted upon, *activate God's power*. The many *promises* of God found in His Word are *conditional*, and they often depend upon the *actions* we must take. Although God has given much revelation to the church, we must learn how to *activate* these precious promises. Jesus has done all that He is going to do. He said, "It is finished" (John 19:30). I must reemphasize this truth. The debt has been paid. The work of the cross is perfect and complete. Now, let's find out what *we must do!*

If ye know these things, happy are ye if ye do them.

John 13:17

We can and must bring the *truth of salvation, healing,* and *deliverance* back to the church and to all in need. We must no longer accept the burden of pain and suffering ourselves. Jesus was *punished* in your place so you could be *forgiven,* and He was wounded so you could be healed and walk in divine health every day of your life.

The promises of God are conditional and must be activated!

Stop! Let's meditate on the above together!

Neck Injury Healed

The following testimony demonstrates that *miracles happen in the now*, without having to wait for some future time. Sometimes, the Holy Spirit will reveal a Word of Knowledge prior to the manifestation of a miracle.

During a time of prayer, the Holy Spirit showed me a white neck brace, which alerted me that He wanted to heal someone with a neck injury. The next day, I saw a woman with a white neck brace, which she wore due to an injury suffered in a car accident.

Embrace the truth of the cross and all that is yours today!

Remembering that I had seen this neck brace in the spirit the day before, I knew that the Lord wanted to perform a miracle. After sharing with her what the Lord had shown me, she gladly received prayer. She later told me that she went home afterward and removed the neck brace—discovering that she had been completely healed. Although she had been unable to return to work previously, she shared that she had indeed returned with no pain.

Today, many are crying out to God to heal and help them yet still remain without their miracle. Why is this, when the Word of God, as we have seen, declares that all that we need is ours to receive today? Let's make the following confession of faith out loud as we continue to seek more of the truth together.

Confession of Faith

Lord Jesus, Your Word clearly says that You have already done all that is necessary for me to receive my miracle today. I'm so grateful that You never turned anyone away who came to You for help. So I ask You now, to help me fully understand and put into practice the truth through divine revelation. In Your name, I pray. Amen.

Miracles are happening here and around the world today!

Second Revelation:
Healing Is For You Today

Miracles are still happening today, and I expect to receive my miracle as well, as I continue to seek greater understanding through revelation of *the truth* of God's Word!

God is our refuge and strength, a very present help in trouble.

Psalms 46:1

Chapter Review!

1. Jesus is still the same *today*, performing many miracles around the world.
2. Every *promise* and *provision* of God is mine to receive today.
3. Jesus has done *everything* He's going to do. Now, I'm going to learn what I need to do to receive my miracle.

For the Lord is good; his mercy is everlasting; And his truth endureth to all generations.

Psalms 100:5

Stop! It's important that you meditate on the entire chapter until its truths become revelation in your spirit before going on. Know that God has a miracle for you today. There is no need to wait!

Are you ready? In the next chapter, let's find out how to *believe* for your miracle!

Chapter 3

Believing For Your Miracle

If ye have faith as a grain of mustard seed, ye shall say unto this mountain, remove hence to yonder place; and it shall remove; and nothing shall be impossible unto you.

Matthew 17:20

As we will see, having the *faith to believe* is a prerequisite, and absolutely necessary, if we are to enjoy the blessings of God promised in His Word. We must allow our faith to rise to the point where we can believe and receive whatever we need. Remember, everything that comes from God must be *received by revelation* of the Holy Spirit *through faith*. Let's consider now what it really means to *believe*.

Your miracle is yours to receive today by faith!

Believing the Gospel

Looking back at my childhood, I am grateful for parents who instilled in me, through regularly attending church, a love and respect for God. I grew up hearing the Gospel and believing that God's Son died for *everyone* on the cross. I believed this truth without question. However, I would learn years later that believing the Gospel Truth was not enough. What truth about God did I lack that would enable me to have an *intimate relationship* with Him?

Do I Have Enough Faith?

Jesus often spoke of one's faith, commending those for their faith and rebuking others for a *lack of faith* or *little faith*. To the centurion who implored Jesus to heal his servant and said, "Speak the word only," Jesus replied, "I have not found so *great faith* in all of Israel. Go thy way, and as thou hast believed, so be it done unto thee" (Matthew 8:8–13). The *good news* is that God has given each of us a *measure of faith* so that we can believe for our miracle too (Romans 12:3).

Real faith expects to receive what you need when you pray!

Be it unto you according to your faith.

Matthew 9:29

Thy faith hath made thee whole.

Mark 5:34

As it is written, the just shall live by faith.

Romans 1:17

For we walk by faith, not by sight.

2 Corinthians 5:7

Stop! Let's take time to meditate and even memorize these scriptures!

What Does It Mean To Believe?

The word *believe* means to be *persuaded*, to place confidence in, or trust. Again, as we proceed, we must be confident in *the truth* of God's Word, for Jesus said of the Father, "Sanctify them through thy truth: thy word is truth" (John 17:17). So, as we place our confidence in the Word of God, let's consider for a moment the word faith. We need faith so we can believe for our miracle.

The truth is that many people think they are walking or believing in faith, but in reality, are far from doing so. Real faith is not presumption or optimism, and it is not a "hope so" mentality. "I hope God will answer my prayers. I hope God will heal me."

What Is Faith?

Hebrews 11:1

You have all the faith you need to experience your miracle!

Faith assures us of things we *expect* and convinces us of the existence of things we cannot see.

Faith is the *assurance* of the reality of tangible things that we have yet to physically see, but that do exist in the realm of the spirit.

Faith is the *certainty* of that which belongs to us, even though we cannot see it.

Faith is the *conviction*, the undisputable proof that we have that which we cannot see.

Faith is based on something real that *already exists* in the spirit realm, but it must be brought into the physical realm to be seen.

Release your faith where the will of God is known!

Faith must *ignore* our *natural* senses and believe what God has said. If you consider God's Word true, you cannot accept your natural senses as evidence.

Faith brings the *invisible* into existence.

Faith is the conviction that what we believe has *already* taken place in the spirit realm, and it can and will be manifested in the natural realm.

Faith is the *substance* of what we hope for or expect; the certainty that the miracle is ours, ready for the taking.

Stop! Meditate until you have the revelation of what faith really is in your spirit!

Remember, it is necessary for us to revisit any truth *many times* until it becomes a revelation in our spirit. This is why it is important that you spend much time meditating as you proceed through each chapter.

Expect Your Miracle

Believing faith is *expectation. When we pray*, we must expect without a doubt that what we ask we will receive before it is manifested in the natural. When we believe and expect God to fulfill His promises, this pleases Him, for the Bible says, "Without faith, it is impossible to please God" (Hebrews 11:6).

Unbelief can keep you from receiving your miracle!

Beware of Unbelief

Unlike faith, unbelief is a major barrier to receiving your miracle. When we question what God has said in His Word, and when we allow doubt to enter our hearts, we are actually bringing *His integrity* regarding His promises and His power to save, heal, and deliver into question. Unbelief, therefore, suggests that God is *not trustworthy*, and, therefore, we must see *unbelief as sin*, which separates us from God and hinders our prayers (Isaiah 59:2).

Unbelief is generally a *choice* we make. If a person wants to believe, but something within keeps them from doing so, nothing will change until *repentance* is made and unbelief is confessed and renounced as sin. However, when a person *refuses to believe*, this may indicate that there is a *spirit of unbelief* in control of one's will to believe.

A Father's Cry for Help

Let's pause for a moment and consider the following story found in Mark 9:21–24. Here we see a desperate father seeking healing for his son.

"And he asked his father, 'How long is it ago since this came unto him?' And he said, 'Of a child. And ofttimes it hath cast him into the fire, and into the waters, to destroy him: but if thou canst do anything, have compassion on us, and help us.' Jesus said unto him, *'If thou canst believe, all things are possible to him that believeth.'* And straightway the father of the child cried out, and said with tears, *'Lord, I believe; help thou mine unbelief.'*"

When you choose to believe, you will receive!

Yes, Jesus will help you too. Right now, if there is any doubt in your heart, take a moment here to pray *out loud!*

Let's Pray!

Father, I do repent and renounce all doubt and unbelief, and I ask You to forgive me for questioning Your Word. I am fully persuaded that You will do what You have said, and I now choose to believe so that I can receive my miracle. In Jesus's name, I pray. Amen.

Being Fully Convinced

Let every man be fully persuaded in his own mind.

Romans 14:5

We have already established the fact that it is God's will to meet your every need today, and therefore, you should be expecting your miracle now! Although, often what we ask for is manifested over a period of time, such as with a physical healing which is progressive, we also know that miracles occur in an instant. Nevertheless, God's promises are *yes and amen* (2 Corinthians 1:20) for the *present time*, and we must continue with complete confidence to expect and believe that we will receive what we need today. Again, this is *expectant faith*.

Too many people are living with a future mentality: *"I hope and pray my miracle will happen someday at God's appointed time."* We must remember that "Behold, now is the day of salvation" (2 Corinthians 6:2), which includes every provision of God—forgiveness of sin, safety, healing, prosperity, and deliverance from every form of bondage. Everything you need, God wants to provide for you today!

For all the promises of God in him are yea, and in him Amen, unto the glory of God.

2 Corinthians 1:20

Stop! Meditate once again until this truth is imprinted deeply upon your heart.

This is where many miss their miracle. You must understand and receive this *revelation of faith* so you can *believe* and *expect* your miracle *today!*

A Daily Decision

Choose to believe God's Word and release your faith for your miracle!

We must choose to make the decision to *believe what God says* in the same way that we choose to make many decisions in our everyday lives. When you make a decision about anything, you decide or choose *what* you are going to do and *when* you are going to do it. Your faith also brings things that *cannot be seen* into something that can be seen in the *natural, now*. In the salvation experience, we see this truth exemplified.

The New Birth

You must put your confident trust in God without doubting!

Many years ago, on June 27, 1975, after hearing that I could know that heaven is my home by placing my faith in Jesus Christ as Savior and Lord—on a particular day, time, and place of *my choosing*, I invited Jesus to come into my heart and life. I was miraculously *born again* as I acknowledged my sin and received God's *free gift of eternal life* through the *shed blood* of His Son.

In the same way, as you *release your faith* right now, every promise of God can be yours as well. Whatever you need, choose with expectation to make this your day, time, and place to *receive your miracle*. Why wait? Today is your day!

Nevertheless, please remember that *most healings are progressive* over a period of time, so don't allow yourself to be discouraged. It was four weeks of standing against arthritic pain that attacked my body before my healing was manifested. (I will be sharing my personal testimony later.) If you will *not doubt*, your miracle will manifest as well.

Stop. Meditate on the fact that you can receive your miracle right now!

We Have Believed Satan's Lies!

"Ye are of your father the devil, and the lusts of your father ye will do. He was a murderer from the beginning, and abode not in the truth, because there is no truth in him."

John 8:44

What Are Some of His Lies?

Satan says, "Don't you know that God *doesn't do miracles* anymore?" Or "Just wait a while. Maybe God will answer your prayers someday *if it's His will*," as if your miracle is *perhaps* somewhere in your future. "I guess it's just not God's time for my miracle yet. Maybe God is allowing me to suffer right now to *teach me a lesson* and make me more like His Son Jesus." This is not *scriptural truth*. We must dispel this false teaching once and for all!

God's Promise for You

God is all-knowing and knows everything about you, and because of His great love for you, He is ready and willing to meet all your needs *right now*! In the Gospels, Jesus never told anyone to *wait to be healed or delivered*. We must remember that Jesus responded *immediately* with great compassion to the suffering of all who came to Him in *faith*.

Don't let Satan's lies keep you from your miracle!

> *When even was come, they brought unto him many that were possessed with devils: and he cast out the spirits with his word, and healed all that were sick: that it might be fulfilled which was spoken by Isaiah the prophet, saying, "Himself took our infirmities and bare our sicknesses."*
>
> *Matthew 8:16-17*

> *"Who his own self bare our sins in his own body on the tree, that we, being dead to sins, should live unto righteousness; by whose stripes ye were healed."*
>
> *1 Peter 2:24*

Yes, Jesus was wounded so that we could be healed and set free from every attack of the enemy. Claim what you need today. Believe it and confess this truth daily.

Walking in Divine Health

As I have previously shared, since receiving the revelation that Jesus purchased divine health and has made every provision for us, I expect to walk in perfect health each and every day. I *continue to resist* painful circumstances, symptoms, or tormenting thoughts and emotions that may occur on a daily basis. As you too resist the enemy and persevere as

Use your authority over every sickness and unacceptable situation!

long as it takes, God's promises for peace, health, wholeness, and every provision are yours to claim every day.

Remember, it is a known fact that people who experience a miracle *exercise their faith.* They do not just wait passively, but they make *a decision to believe,* as they *wait expectantly to receive* what they need. You must do the same.

Stop! Let's meditate on this important truth!

Healed of Prostate Cancer

The following testimony is an example of this truth. While attending a Bible study group, after sharing a couple of testimonies of miracles that had recently occurred in our healing ministry, I perceived in my spirit that a man who was present had faith to believe for his healing miracle. After laying hands on him and praying the *prayer of faith,* according to James 5:13–15, he felt the power of God go through his body and testified that he believed he was healed.

Desiring confirmation, two days later he returned to his doctor and requested that a test for prostate cancer be repeated. The test confirmed his miracle—there was now no indication of cancer in the prostate. This true story confirms the *biblical truth* that when we release our faith, miracles, which are in the *spirit realm, will manifest in the natural realm now.*

Use Your Authority!

Through the Holy Spirit, every believer in Christ has been given power and authority over every sickness and unacceptable situation. There are decisions we must make if we want *God's best*. We should expect to *live healthily* and never get sick, standing ready every day to resist the enemy's attempts to bring illness and harmful circumstances

Always receive God's best and never settle for less!

into our lives. To do less is a blatant *disregard, disrespect, and devaluing* of Christ's sacrifice and the work of the cross which purchased salvation, healing, and deliverance for all.

I have set before you life and death...therefore, choose life.

Deuteronomy 30:19

No More Migraine Headaches

The following testimony confirms the power we have been given when we *exercise* our God-given authority over all the power of the enemy (Luke 10:19).

Marie came to my home for healing prayer. She had suffered with ongoing migraine headaches for years. Having attended deliverance classes, she had become aware of the source of her pain, a spirit of migraines. Marie was anointed with oil. As I took *authority* over this spirit of infirmity in Jesus's name, the pain would move to different locations in the head.

God has promised to supply your every need!

When this occurs, it is evident that a spirit is present and that it must be cast out. Though there was some resistance, when this spirit was renounced all pain did leave. Marie had *received her miracle!*

Stop! Let's meditate on this for a moment!

Needs or Wants?

At this point, let's make a distinction between what we *need* and what we *want*. Like our Heavenly Father, as a parent we would not withhold from our children what they need like food, shelter, and daily care. However, sometimes we may withhold what they want because we know it would not be in their best interest.

In the same way, our basic needs of health, general well-being, and daily provision God will not withhold from His children. "But my God shall supply all your need according to His riches in glory by Christ Jesus" (Philippians 4:19). Therefore, we too should *diligently seek* to receive all that has been provided for us now, which is my heart's desire for you.

Whatsoever ye shall ask in my name, that will I do, that the Father may be glorified in the Son. If ye shall ask anything in my name, I will do it.

John 14:13-14

As we continue, join me in declaring the following confession with a heart full of faith *out loud.*

Confession of Faith

Father, I declare that today I make a decision to believe with total confidence for my miracle. No more lack! No more losses! No more bondage and no more sickness in Jesus's name! I fully expect You to do what only You can do, for with You *nothing is impossible* (Luke 1:37).

I choose to release my faith and believe for Your touch in every area of my life. I declare I am free! I renounce the works of satan and his kingdom, and I believe that today, I receive Your very best for my life in Jesus's mighty name, I pray. Amen.

(Continue to make this declaration daily naming each need.)

What Others Have Said About Faith

Faith receives the promises, embraces, and comforts the soul unspeakably with it.

—John Bunyan

All that you need is in the realm of the Spirit!

Believe that when you come into the presence of God, you can have all you came for. You can take it away, and you can use it, for all the power of God is at your disposal in response to your faith.

—Smith Wigglesworth

Faith sees the invisible, believes the unbelievable, and receives the impossible.

—Corrie Ten Boom

It's not a matter of what Jesus can do, but of what you can believe!

—Kenneth E. Hagin, Sr.

We must wrap our need with expectation and declare the manifestation of our miracle. Today is your day!

—Benny Hinn

Stop! Let's take a moment to meditate on the above!

Your Miracle Is in the Spirit Realm

Believe the unbelievable and receive the impossible!

As just mentioned, this truth is so important. We must understand that everything we need is already done in the realm of the Spirit—waiting for faith to be exercised in order for a miracle to manifest in the material world. Therefore, as a child of God, your blessing awaits only your *faith to activate it*. Now is the time to receive your blessings because faith is in the present. Jesus has done everything He's going to do. Once again, He said, "It is finished" (John 19:30). These things are waiting for *us to decide* when we are going to claim them. God has placed within us the ability to determine *what we will believe and when we will receive.*

Stop! Meditate on the importance of this truth!

You may be thinking at this point, *Wait a minute! Doesn't God have His appointed time for my miracle? That's what I've been taught.* Yes, the Lord knows all things. He knows every detail of your life and that moment in time when your miracle will happen. However, this truth does not suggest that you need or should expect to wait. We must expect to receive what we need each and every day. Remember, "Now is the accepted time; behold, now is the day of salvation" (2 Corinthians 6:2). Again, this includes your healing, your deliverance from all that holds you in bondage, and every *provision of blessing.*

Third Revelation: Revelation of Faith

Expectant faith believes you have already received your miracle *when you pray* and *before it manifests* itself in the natural. Faith believes and expects God to fulfill His promises today!

There's no need to wait.

Today is your day!

Chapter Review!

1. My *faith to believe* is the *key* to my miracle.
2. Believing means being *fully persuaded* that when I pray with expectant faith, according to God's promises, *what I believe I will receive.*
3. I will no longer believe satan's lies, but rather *seek and embrace* God's truth. All of my needs God wants to provide for me *today.*
4. All that I need is already in the realm of the Spirit. As I *release my faith*, my miracle is *activated* and will manifest itself in the physical realm.
5. I need to *thank God* for my miracle and *stop asking* Him to do what He has already done.

If thou canst believe, all things are possible to him that believeth.

—Mark 9:23

Stop! If you still are unsure about the *revelation of faith*, go back and meditate on this chapter before going on, until this truth becomes a revelation in your spirit.

As we continue to diligently seek the truth, let's consider how you can r*eceive* your miracle *today!*

Chapter 4

Receiving Your Miracle

*Hitherto have ye asked nothing in my name;
Ask, and ye shall receive, that your joy may be full.*

—*John 16:24*

As we continue, I pray that the Lord will open your spiritual eyes and ears so that the revelations we've been discussing become *light* and *life* to your spirit. We need to see and hear something over and over in order to fully grasp and experience its meaning. You'll find much repetition in this chapter and *frequent review* as you read and reread passages, which will deepen your faith and understanding. Allow the light of God's Word to invade your spirit as the Holy Spirit brings fresh revelation.

Your miracle must be received by faith!

Another Key!

Another very important key to your miracle is understanding that although God's gifts are free, each must be *received by faith* as you would receive any other gift. Simply put, in order to receive your miracle, you must *believe it is yours*, as we have already discussed, and then make that confession of faith *daily until your prayers are answered.*

It's Your Decision

We have emphasized that living a prosperous, healthy life is a *decision* we must make every day. This means we must *stand against* any attempt of the enemy to bring harm to our lives. Once we walk in this truth, you will find that '*it is easier to live in divine health*' than it is to receive a healing. Let's ponder this statement for a moment.

Every provision has already been made for you!

Remember that it is God's will to keep you in perfect health as a way of life, and He can make it possible for us to never get sick. You say *impossible!* Nevertheless, know that there are those who have testified that this is very true in their lives. They do not accept symptoms of illness, and should any try to manifest, they are resisted with all authority in Jesus's name.

The wounds Jesus took on the cross in our place made this possible. The thought just occurred to me that Scripture never suggests that Jesus was ever sick, so let's not ever settle for less than *God's best!*

Today, many are crying out to God for their miracle but fail to comprehend that everything that comes from God has already been provided—but again, every promise of God *must be received* by faith!

What Does It Mean To Receive?

To receive, you must take into your possession that which is given to you or delivered to you as a gift.

Isn't it true that you can obtain a gift with your name on it, but unless you open the gift and use its contents, it will not truly become yours to enjoy? In the same way, what you need from God must be *possessed* by you as a free gift. Could this be why so many *prayers go unanswered* and many remain sick among us? You need to grasp this revelation that as you believe and expect your miracle, you must receive it and *possess* it by faith as well.

Every promise of God is yours to possess by faith!

> *Stop!* Meditate on this for a while.
> This truth is a major key to your miracle!

Faith That Receives

Before I was *born again*, though I loved God and believed the Gospel, I had no assurance of salvation. I struggled for a long time until by *revelation* I came to understand that you can know all about Christ, even serve Him, and not be saved from the penalty of sin. I needed to *not only believe* the Gospel but *receive this precious gift* of eternal life for myself through faith in the shed *blood of Jesus Christ.*

Make a decision to experience divine health every day!

> *For by grace are ye saved through faith; and that not of yourselves: it is the gift of God: not of works, lest any man should boast.*
>
> Ephesians 2:8–9

But the simple truth that escaped me was, *How do you get saved or receive Jesus Christ?* Sound simple? At the time it wasn't to me. However, I later learned that all I had to do was repent of my sin and invite Jesus into my heart and life—telling Him that *I made a decision to receive* Him as my Savior and Lord through a *simple prayer*. What could be simpler than that?

At this point, I want to suggest to you that *receiving what you need today* is just as *simple*. If you talk to anyone who has received a miracle, a healing, or a deliverance of some kind, they will assure you *after the fact* that it was so simple—that what God had done for them He would do for you.

> *Stop!* Take time here to meditate on what you just read. We see that in order to be saved, healed, or to receive anything from God, we must believe and receive every precious gift by faith!

Believe and Receive

At a particular time, on a specific day, you can, after hearing and believing the Gospel message, make a decision to accept and receive God's free gift of eternal life. Then, acting on that belief, choose to speak to God in prayer in order to receive His Son Jesus as Savior and Lord. From that moment,

Confess your miracle with faith-filled actions!

through the *new birth experience*, according to the Word of God, you are spiritually *born again*—now a new creation in Christ; "old things are passed away; behold, and *all things are become new*" (2 Corinthians 5:17).

In the same way, you can, at a moment in time of *your choosing*, believe and receive every provision of God with expectant faith, as you make a decision to receive all that God has for you.

For faith to be effective, it must be *confessed*, and *actions* should be taken to receive your miracle. As you do what you couldn't do before, your faith-filled actions will cause your miracle to manifest.

Believing As You Wait

Let me point out here again that as we release our faith, the answer may or may not necessarily occur immediately. Most physical healings take place over a period of time and are progressive. Nevertheless, we must continue to believe, receive, and declare what God has promised. Stand firm against anything that contradicts what God has said. *Your miracle is here for the taking!*

Even though physical symptoms or painful circumstances may persist, don't give up regardless of what you *see or feel*. Keep your confession until what you need is received. Boldly declare, *"I'm healed, delivered, and set free, and I believe I will receive my miracle today!"*

Believing and acting upon the truth will bring forth your miracle. Faith is loosed by our *confession* and manifested through our *actions*. When faith is released and acted upon, miracles happen.

> *Stop*! Let's meditate! What actions can you take by faith that will activate your miracle?

Faith in Action

There are many examples of people's lives in the Bible who received divine intervention. In each case, faith was released, and steps were taken to receive the promises of God.

Your faith will activate your miracle!

By faith, Noah built an ark, and he and his family were protected from the waters that covered the earth.

(Genesis 6–8)

By faith, the children of Israel followed Moses and were delivered from the hand of Pharaoh.

(Exodus 3–14)

By faith, Ruth left her home and family and found love and acceptance with the people of God.

(Ruth 1–4)

By faith, Esther risked her life and saved her people, the Jews, from extinction.

(Esther 8)

By faith, Joshua obeyed God, the walls of Jericho were destroyed, and Israel possessed the Promised Land.

(Joshua 1–2)

By faith, Jesus went to the cross and purchased redemption for all who would believe in Him.

(Luke 23–24)

The Healing of a Blind Man

In Luke 18:35–43, we read the account of a blind man who cried out, "Jesus, thou Son of David, have mercy on me." Jesus replied, "What wilt thou that I shall do unto thee?" "Lord, that I may receive my sight." Jesus said unto him: "Receive thy sight: *thy faith hath saved thee*." And immediately, he received his sight.

Here is an example of a man who asked for a miracle but also took action and received it by faith. Jesus commended this man's faith—declaring that it was his faith that had made him well.

A Healing of Infirmity

We see in the scriptures this same scenario with the woman who had an issue of blood. She took action as she touched the hem of Jesus's garment and was immediately healed. "Daughter, thy faith hath made thee whole; go in peace, and be whole of thy plague." (Mark 5:25–43)

Release your faith with expectation until your miracle manifests!

A Common Mistake

I cannot emphasize this enough! All too often, many are crying out to God, *hoping for a miracle*, while often relying on another's faith and prayers. Yet, they fail to release their *own faith* to receive what they need themselves. Take a moment here to pray and purpose in your heart not to let this happen to you.

Stop! Do take time to meditate here once again!

Symptoms Disappear

I heard recently about a man who suddenly began to experience symptoms of muscular sclerosis. After crying out to God for healing, as he continued to wait for his miracle, the Lord spoke to him. *"Stop asking me to heal you. I already have! Now I want you to thank me for perfect health!"* This revelation transformed his thinking, and in a short time, as he obeyed God's Word, every symptom left, and he was completely healed.

What can we learn from this man's experience? Perhaps it's time that we too begin to *thank the Lord* for what He has *already done*—declaring that we believe we have perfect health and all that we need. This being the case, I now join my faith with yours and believe with you for your miracle.

Expectant Faith

When you are expecting company to arrive for dinner, you are not hoping your guests will come. You expect them to arrive at the appointed time as planned, and when they appear, you receive them into your home with joy. In the same way, put your faith into action and begin to see yourself healed—every situation turned around and every need supplied.

He that doeth truth cometh to the light…

John 3:12

Resist and Receive

Once again, though your miracle can occur suddenly, remember that often you must declare your need as you *resist symptoms and renounce circumstances* that you may be experiencing over a period of time. Nevertheless, continue to stand in faith until health and well-being return. Let me give you an example.

Resist every symptom of illness and renounce every unacceptable circumstance!

A Personal Testimony

As stated earlier, I have learned to refuse to allow sickness or unacceptable circumstances to affect my life adversely. Therefore, when these occur, I immediately *resist and renounce* them until they are gone. I know they have no place in my life according to Scripture.

Jesus already took in His own body our pain and sickness, paying the price for all our suffering in every circumstance of our lives.

Attack of Pain

As an example of this truth—one morning, as I arose from my bed to begin my day, I felt a sharp pain in my knee and later in several other places in my body. I could hardly walk. The pain was severe. Like you, I had two choices. I could accept the pain, see a doctor, which I have done through most of my life, or I could *use the authority* God has given me

Remember faith expects your miracle before it manifests in the natural!

and command the pain to leave in the name of Jesus. I chose the latter. I immediately and *persistently* began to take authority over the pain, and although a battle ensued, in a short amount of time, I was totally healed. What am I saying?

If I had not *resisted* the arthritic pain, I would still be suffering today and would probably be even worse. Like most people, I would continue to go to the doctor, but eventually, the arthritis would progress with little relief. However, because I know that no pain, sickness, or disease have any place in my life, I chose to *stand in faith* until all the pain was gone. Divine health is *mine for the taking* as it is for you! (Psalm 91:10)

Resist With Authority

What does it mean to resist? The word "resist" means to withstand that which opposes or affects our lives adversely. As we have discussed before, we know that Satan seeks to bring harm to our lives in many ways—including sickness and the various trials of life. Again, we must use the power and authority God has given us to resist the enemy every day. We will discuss this further in a later chapter.

Continue To Stand!

In the past, when sickness, pain, or problems would occur, we may or may not have prayed to God for help. However, remember that God has done all He's going to do! He has already provided *all that we need*. We must never accept anything that is harmful to us or that tries to come against us without resistance. Unfortunately, not having known *the truth* throughout most of our lives, we have probably accepted these things far too long.

Receive the revelation that according to the Word of God, Jesus purchased the forgiveness of your sins with His blood and your healing, divine health, and deliverance with the whipping He endured and the wounds He received in His own body through His death on the cross. When we don't resist boldly with all of our being, we are allowing the enemy to steal, kill, and destroy many of our blessings.

Boldly stand until your miracle manifests!

Stop! Meditate! Lay hold of this important truth until it becomes revelation for you!

Needless Suffering

Could this be the reason so many continue to suffer needlessly today, even after crying out to God for their miracle? We must no longer be complacent but rather "Fight the good fight of faith" (I Timothy 6:12) and believe and receive what may seem impossible!

May God grant us the resolve, strength, and courage to do our part so that we may walk in all that Jesus purchased for us on the cross. When we don't, let's not make His sacrifice of no effect and His suffering to be in vain. God forbid!

Stop! Meditate for this truth is key to your miracle!

Just Three Steps

With *expectant faith* and *true repentance* of heart as you renounce all sin, the way to obtain your miracle is seen in the following steps:

As you put into practice these steps you will receive your miracle!

1. *Believ*e the revelation of the Word of God.
2. *Respond* to the revelation of the Word of God by:
    - *Resisting* every symptom of illness and all harmful circumstances.
    - *Declaring* what the Word of God says that you are healed, whole, and set free in every area of your life.
    - *Releasing* your faith as you boldly take back what has been stolen from you by the enemy—taking the appropriate and

necessary actions that will activate your miracle. Ask the Holy Spirit to guide you in doing what you didn't or couldn't do before.
- *Claiming* as a believer and follower of Jesus Christ your rightful *inheritance* in Him as you believe for salvation, divine health, and deliverance from all torment and oppression.
3. Expect results and *receive* the manifestation of your miracle!

Stop! Meditate here and digest the truth
that can set you completely free!

Let's Pray!

Father, I pray for each one who needs a miracle today, whether it be financial, relational, physical, mental, emotional, or spiritual, and I ask that You hear the cry of every heart. Thank You for giving to us *the truth* and for providing salvation, healing, and deliverance through the death of Your son, Jesus. In His name, I pray. Amen.

Confession of Faith

Right now, if you would like to express your faith in the Lord Jesus and receive His touch for your miracle, I invite you to pray with me *out loud!*

Dear Jesus, I come just as I am, believing and trusting in Your love and mercy. I invite You into every area of my life. I surrender to You and declare that I now receive You as my Lord and Savior. I am sorry for my sins. Please forgive me, and as You have forgiven me, I now forgive everyone who has hurt me, as well. I repent and renounce all my sin and ask You to cleanse me of all unrighteousness. (1 John 1:9)

I give no place to any loss suffered, any bondage, sickness, disease, pain, or spirit of infirmity, and I command these things to go right now in Your name. I receive my miracle (name it) by faith without doubting, and I declare my body, soul, mind, and spirit, and every area of my life to be whole and well. I now confess I am saved through Your shed blood, and I am healed, and set free by Your stripes for the glory of God. Amen.

(Continue to make this confession
daily until every need is fulfilled)

Fourth Revelation: Receiving Your Miracle

Every gift from God must be received as you would receive any other gift—with expectant faith in what God has said in His Word!

Chapter Review!

1. I must consciously make a decision to receive my miracle.
2. Everything from God must be received by faith.
3. Real faith does not hope for a miracle.
4. Faith expects a miracle before it is seen in the natural.
5. When I act upon this truth and release my faith, miracles happen.

"And all things, whatsoever you ask in prayer, believing, you shall receive."

— *Matthew 21:22*

Stop! Continue to meditate on this chapter until every truth becomes revelation for you!

In the next chapter, because some have lost their miracle, let's discuss what we must *know and do* to ensure this doesn't happen to you!

Chapter 5

Keeping Your Miracle

*For we are made partakers of Christ,
if we hold the beginning of our confidence
steadfast unto the end.*

— Hebrews 3:14

It's true that one can receive a miracle in a healing service or at any time or any place where faith has been released. But sometimes afterward, doubt and uncertainty can open the door for symptoms and circumstances to try and return. As long as Satan has the freedom to continue to torment us without resistance, the battle for our *full inheritance* of divine health and freedom in Christ will continue.

There's no need to lose your miracle when you know the truth that will set you free!

Satan wants to steal, kill, and destroy all that belongs to you. We must remember that every day of our lives, there is a war raging between good and evil. The enemy will try to attack your mind with lies in order to steal your miracle. We must take captive every thought and refuse to allow *doubt and unbelief* to take over our thought-life (2 Corinthians 10:5).

Without having a firm understanding of the truth of God's Word and its revelations on healing and deliverance, instead of standing in faith and resisting the enemy, many have *lost their miracle* by failing to do so. Symptoms of ill health and difficult circumstances are allowed to return *without resistance.*

A Miracle is Lost

The following testimony is an example of such a loss. During one of our healing seminars, a woman who had suffered for several years with tinnitus or ringing in the ears, received her miracle. Throughout the day, she rejoiced as she shared her miracle with family and friends. However, during the night when she awoke, ringing had returned. As she resisted, the ringing left once again. In the morning, though she continued to command the ringing to go, *growing discouraged*, she gave up, and her miracle was lost.

What went wrong? Understand that if she had persisted in faith, she would still be healed today. But because she had *not been taught* and prepared that this might occur, doubt crept in, and she failed to persevere, allowing symptoms to return. What must we learn from this real-life situation? This tragedy is being repeated over and over, as we have already shared. This is why it is imperative that "the truth be told and shouted from the rooftops!" God has given us all that we need to know—but again, many are *perishing for a lack of this knowledge* (Hosea 4:6).

This is why *Waves of Glory Miracle Ministries* is dedicated to bringing *the truth* to all who are suffering needlessly. We believe the Lord will use this book, which He commissioned, this ministry, and many others like it, to bring healing and deliverance to His church and beyond. God wants everyone walking in divine health and wholeness in every area of our lives. As a believer in Christ, it is your *birthright*. Isn't it time that we truly walk in all that is ours through the cross of Calvary? I say, enough is enough! How about you?

You must *hold on to your miracle* by releasing your own faith—resisting every harmful symptom and circumstance. The enemy will surely try to steal your miracle if you let him.

Stop! Meditate on this important truth!

Reasons Why Some Have Lost Their Miracle

The following are some of the reasons why healings are lost and harmful situations are allowed to return:

Don't allow anything to steal your miracle!

1. When a miracle is received through *another's faith* rather than our own. We need to boldly resist any work of the enemy *ourselves* with confident faith.
2. When the enemy is given access or the *legal right* to our lives because of sin, which opens the door to his attack. Through repentance, all access is denied.
3. When we speak a *wrong confession* of sickness and problems with our words, rather than words of faith based on what God's Word says. Your words can bring death or life to your situation.
4. Where there is *no understanding or awareness of oppressive spirits*, which seek to destroy, and *no action* is taken *to resist* them. We must become knowledgeable about deliverance ministry.
5. When we just don't know. Yes, sometimes there may seem to be no explanation! Here, we must rely on the sovereignty of God, who knows all things and in whom we can safely trust (Psalm 37:3–4).

Stop! It's important that you meditate on the above!

Another True Story

There was a man born with a club foot that was turned in and one leg was shorter than the other. This man received a creative miracle during a healing service. After *six months*, however, as he was walking down the sidewalk, suddenly his foot turned in as before. He had two choices: accept the loss of his miracle or stand firm in his faith.

Instead of believing, *Well, I guess I wasn't really healed after all*, knowing the truth, he said, "Devil, you can't put that back on me. I won't accept it." Immediately, his foot returned to normal, and he went on his way rejoicing! Does this sound too simple to be true? Let's read on.

When we accept the doctor's report and symptoms of illness or bad news of any kind without resistance, we are giving satan the *legal right* to oppress and torment us. *You're really sick, so just accept it. There's no hope for your family and you're never going to get out of debt.*

We must declare, "My God will do this because nothing is impossible for those who believe" (Mark 9:23). God's Word says that divine health and all that we need is ours to possess as we have already discussed (Philippians 4:19).

You must boldly resist the work of the enemy!

We must remember that when symptoms or unacceptable circumstances try to return, we must *speak* what God's Word says—*resist*, and *renounce* what we know is not God's will. We must stand against what the enemy is trying to do until all is *restored*! Though it may take a while, be assured your miracle will return. Be encouraged! Be *firm and consistent*, and believe and expect your miracle today!

Stop! Meditate here for a moment!

A Personal Testimony

Recently, after having *experienced two healings* myself, it is a fact that symptoms have tried to return on several occasions. However, because I know that the enemy will often try to return with previous symptoms, I immediately resisted, and each time they left. I pray this will be your experience as well. Sickness, pain, or loss of any kind can have no place in your life. If you will *resist*, the Lord will keep you in perfect health and free of torment, which is clearly yours to enjoy.

How Do I Resist?

You will find below *statements or declarations* which you can *speak out loud* as you take authority over symptoms and circumstances which have no place in your life. Boldly and firmly bind any attempt of the enemy to steal your healing or oppress you in any way.

When *doubt* comes, say, "Doubt, I resist you, In Jesus's Name! I Refuse To Doubt!"

When *fear* comes, speak to it, "Fear, I resist you, In Jesus's Name! I Refuse To Fear!"

When *sickness* comes, say, "Sickness, I refuse every symptom. By Jesus's stripes, I am healed! I resist you, In Jesus's Name!"

When *torment* of any kind and oppression come, say, "I command you to go now, In Jesus's Name!"

"Satan, I *renounce* and *bind you*, and I refuse to accept this, In Jesus's Name!"

We must be specific and bind and loose what the enemy is trying to do!

Stop! Meditate here before going on. Become acquainted with the above commands, and begin to use them!

Sin Opens the Door

It's important to note again that when spirits are cast out, they must depart unless some *legal right* remains because of sin. Know that when they do leave, they will begin to seek another place to dwell. If they don't find one, they will often *try to return*.

Don't give the enemy the legal right to steal your miracle!

However, these areas are secure when Jesus is Lord of our lives, and we are free from all sin. When this is true, we have nothing to fear. *Total surrender* of our lives to God is imperative. Otherwise, it won't be long before unclean spirits may come to torment and oppress you once again. Don't let this happen to you!

When the unclean spirit is gone out of a man, he walketh through dry places, seeking rest; and finding none, he saith, 'I will return unto my house whence I came out.' And when he cometh, he findeth it swept and garnished (put in order). Then goeth he, and taketh to him seven other spirits more wicked than himself; and they enter in, and dwell there; and the last state of that man is worse than the first.

Luke 11:24–26

Stop! Let's pause once again and
meditate on the topic above!

You May Be Wondering?

Before continuing, let's consider the following questions!

Question: Why do we pray in the name of Jesus?

Answer: Because there is power and authority in Jesus's name.

Whatsoever ye shall ask in my name, that I will do, that the Father may be glorified in the Son. If ye ask anything in my name, I will do it.

John 14:13–14

That at the name of Jesus every knee shall bow, of things in heaven, and things in earth, and things under the earth; and that every tongue should confess that Jesus Christ is Lord, to the glory of God the Father.

Philippians 2:10–11

Go ye into all the world, and preach the gospel... And these signs shall follow them that believe; In my name shall they cast out devils... they shall lay hands on the sick, and they shall recover.

Mark 16:15–18

Question: Why must we resist satan, also known as the devil?

Answer: Because satan is often the source behind many of your troubles.

> *Submit yourselves therefore to God, resist the devil, and he will flee from you. Draw nigh to God, and he will draw nigh to you.*
>
> James 4:7–8

> *Be sober, be vigilant; because your adversary the devil, as a roaring lion, walketh about, seeking whom he may devour: whom resist steadfast in the faith, knowing that the same afflictions are accomplished in your brethren that are in the world.*
>
> 1 Peter 5:8-9

Question: Why do we bind and loose and cast out demons?

Answer: Because this is how the power of satan is broken.

> *Whatsoever thou shalt bind on earth shall be bound in heaven: and whatsoever thou shalt loose on earth shall be loosed in heaven.*
>
> Matthew 16:19

> *If I (Jesus) cast out devils by the Spirit of God, then the kingdom of God has come unto you.*
>
> Matthew 12:28

Is not this the fast that I have chosen? To loose the bands of wickedness, and to undo the heavy burdens, to let the oppressed go free, and that ye break every yoke?

Isaiah 58:6

Be absolutely convinced by the Word of God!

Stop! Take a moment to meditate here!

Beware of the Thief!

Remember, though the battle rages, if you remain consistent when symptoms or circumstances try to return, they have to go. But you need to be *absolutely convinced* by what the Word says and continue to stand in faith for as long as it takes. However, if you begin to waver in your faith and stop resisting, unbelief will give place to the devil to continue to harass and bring torment. Most likely, things may return as before, and he will successfully have stolen your miracle.

Give no place to the devil.

Ephesians 4:27

The truth is, if you don't have *enough faith* to receive and hold on to your miracle, the devil can and often will steal it from you. There are many who will testify to this fact. When we deny with our words what the Word of God says, we are in *unbelief.*

A Word of Caution!

It has also been noted that testifying of your miracle is very important, and failure to do so has resulted in miracles being lost. Be sure to always share your testimony and give God the glory!

> *And they overcame him by the blood of the Lamb, and by the word of their testimony.*
>
> Revelation 12:11

Share your miracle with others and rejoice!

Many Testify

The wonderful news is that many are testifying that when they *put into practice* the revelations we have been discussing—symptoms, suffering, and circumstances really do turn around and restoration is experienced. I pray that you too will begin to experience the same, as the Holy Spirit imparts the truth to your spirit as well. Let's declare the following together, *out loud!*

Confession of Faith

Lord Jesus, I will believe and receive my miracle, and I renounce any attempt of the devil to steal it from me. If any symptoms or unacceptable circumstances try to return, I will resist them in Jesus's name—for I know divine health and the promises of God are mine to enjoy. I close every door to Satan and remind him that he was defeated at Calvary's cross. Therefore, I will bind any attempt of the enemy to steal what is mine for as long as it takes, in order for my miracle to manifest and remain. Thank You, Lord. In Your precious name, I pray. Amen.

Ready for Battle!

We may have to do battle for a time, but all suffering cannot remain when we believe God's Word and declare what He says and not what you may *see or feel*. Remember, because there is power in the word of our testimony, it is important that we *boldly confess* our miracle so that we may give the glory to Jesus—our healer and deliverer.

Stop! Meditate here before going on!

A Walking Miracle

Before leaving this chapter on "Keeping Your Miracle," I'd like to share another story that I trust will encourage you to continue to fight for your miracle and live a lifestyle of miracles for the glory of God.

Know that the victory has already been won but we must enforce that victory every day!

It was well reported by the media not long ago that a miracle took place when a woman who had been paralyzed for over twenty years, miraculously came out of her wheelchair during a revival meeting and was healed. By the power of the Holy Spirit, she began to have feeling in her legs once again. *Releasing her faith*, she stood up and slowly began to move her legs one step at a time. This healing miracle was videotaped for the whole world to see.

However, I am mentioning this true story in this chapter because you may not know that shortly after, she was once again unable to walk. What happened? As we have shared, it is not uncommon for symptoms to try and return. This has been my experience and many others as well.

Thankfully, she knew enough not to receive what she was seeing and experiencing. As she *resisted Satan's attempt to steal* her miracle, the paralysis once again left, and she was free of this infirmity that had held her in bondage for almost a quarter of a century. Today, she and her husband continue to travel as they share their story and bring hope to people everywhere, who are suffering and in need of a miracle as well.

Fifth Revelation: Keeping Your Miracle

Though sickness or adverse circumstances may try to return, when I actively resist any attempt of the enemy to steal my miracle, victory is assured as I stand firm on the truth of God's Word!

> *Behold, I give unto you power to tread on serpents and scorpions, and over all the power of the enemy; and nothing shall by any means hurt you.*
>
> Luke 10:19

Chapter Review!

1. I must be absolutely convinced and must *stand firm* in my faith in God's Word in order to keep my miracle.
2. If *symptoms or adverse circumstances* try to return, I will strongly resist them and command them to go for as long as it takes—knowing that they have no legal right to remain.
3. I will *give no place* to fear, doubt, or the devil.
4. I will *boldly confess* my miracle and not allow Satan to steal what is mine any longer.
5. I will always give *God the glory* as I share my testimony with others.

Watch and pray, that ye enter not into temptation: the spirit indeed is willing, but the flesh is weak.

Matthew 26:41

Stop! Let's take some additional time to meditate on this important chapter before going on to the next!

Remember, the truths we have been discussing must become revelation for you in your spirit so that you will have the faith to believe, receive, and keep your miracle!

In the next chapter, we will learn how to *confess* with our words what we *believe* in our heart. Let's now discuss the important truth that *your miracle is in your mouth!*

Chapter 6

Your Miracle Is In Your Mouth

*Death and life are in the power of the tongue,
And they that love it will eat the fruit thereof.*

Proverbs 18:21

    The Word of God has much to say about the power that is in your tongue. You must understand that the words we speak, often carelessly, affect our lives. The things we are speaking now will affect our present and our future. When we speak into the atmosphere around us, we cause a change to occur for better or worse.

    Yes, the *power to choose* to speak sickness or health, blessings or problems, is in your mouth. Tragically, most do not know that they have a choice. Today, many are sick and continue to struggle in various ways because they are confessing what they are *experiencing*—rather than what *God's Word says* and what they want to see take place in their lives.

> *"I have set before you life and death, blessing and cursing; therefore choose life, that both thou and thy seed (descendants) may live..."*
>
> *Deuteronomy 30:19*

Miracle Testimonies

Today, many are giving testimony of miracles received when they began to speak what God says in His Word. Whether your words are spoken over yourself or on behalf of others, your words have great power to change circumstances. Again, you must have a *revelation* of this truth in your spirit.

You have been given the power to choose life or death!

The following testimonies are examples of what can happen when we speak the Word of God over our lives.

Healed of Cancer

Recently, I heard Bible teacher Marilyn Hickey share her healing testimony. At one time, she had been diagnosed with cancer. Rather than accept the doctor's report, she went home and began to speak scriptures concerning healing to her body every hour over a period of time. When she went back to her doctor, there was no trace of cancer whatsoever. This is just one example of many such miracles, where the power of speaking God's Word heals and transforms lives. Read on and see how your words can restore life for yourself and others.

Man Comes Out of Coma

Due to a car accident, a man lay in a coma in the hospital that had been declared brain dead. When the Word of God was declared over his body for several days, the man woke up completely healed. What brought about this miracle?

You can be healed and set free by the words of your mouth!

Once again, declaring healing scriptures *out loud* activated God's power. His body was made completely well by the power of the Holy Spirit. Great power is released when the Word of God is spoken with expectant faith. We must hide God's Word in our hearts as we choose to believe it and speak it over our lives (Psalm 119:11).

> *"This book of the law shall not depart out of thy mouth; but thou shalt meditate therein day and night... for then thou shalt make thy way prosperous, and then thou shalt have good success."*
>
> —*Joshua 1:8*

There is a direct correlation between the things we are saying out of our mouth and what occurs in our lives. If we change what we say, we can change people and the world around us. Words have power, for there is no distance in the spirit. We can speak blessings or curses. The Bible says there is the power of life and death in your tongue. May God help us to be careful with our words!

Stop! Let's meditate together on what you just read!

The Realm of the Spirit

Understand that in the realm of the spirit, every provision has already been made for you. Your miracle *awaits the release of your faith*, which will bring its manifestation into the natural realm. God, who is all-knowing, has not been taken by surprise and is well aware of your situation. Therefore, we must begin to call those things we need to ourselves

Declare your miracle with words of faith!

by faith. As we decree something in the name of Jesus, the provision of God is released by the power of God, "calling those things which be not as though they were." (Romans 4:17)

Yes, it's true! Many are waiting for their miracle—not knowing that their miracle is in their mouth. We can speak God's Word out loud and *decree a thing*, and it will be established. Unfortunately, even though we may speak words of faith, all too often we turn around and cancel our faith-filled words with words of *denial and unbelief.*

I Decree and Declare!

> *Thou shalt also decree a thing, and it shall be established unto thee:*
>
> —Job 22:28

Let's boldly speak forth the following declarations on a daily basis—knowing that there is power in our words. Then, we will begin to see God's blessings and favor over our lives.

(Use 'In Jesus's Name' *before* each statement)

1. Every part of my life is blessed (James 1:25).
2. I am blessed physically with divine health, mentally with a sound mind, emotionally with healthy positive feelings, and spiritually with God's Word thru the renewing of my mind (Romans 12:2).
3. I am blessed with financial prosperity and success in all I set my hand to do (Deuteronomy 28:8).
4. I am blessed relationally, interpersonally, and physiologically (Proverbs 28:20).
5. I speak increase over every area of my life, and there is wealth and riches in my house (Psalm 112:3).
6. Today, my life is in direct alignment with the plan and purpose of God and my destiny (Romans 8:28).
7. I speak and receive every good and perfect gift from above into my life for myself, my family, and friends (James 1:17).
8. I am healed and blessed, and I thank you Lord for perfect health and prosperity in every area of my life (3 John 2).

Stop! Take time to pause, meditate, and speak the above declarations!

Powerful Words

Speak God's word and put His Word to the Test!

As a word of testimony, I have found this truth confirmed wherever I go. As I speak what God says in His Word, I have experienced personal healings and miracles for myself and many others. Put God's Word to the test! What He has done for others, He will do for you (Acts 10:34). But you must remain steadfast and thoroughly convinced that what you say, you shall have. May your faith continue to increase and be released as you receive your miracle today! (See Section: "Your Prayers Avail Much")

Let's make the following confession
of faith together, *out loud!*

Confession of Faith

Father, I believe that the words I speak are powerful and can bring life or death to myself and those around me. I purpose in my heart to speak words of life. *I believe and confess* that I am blessed in every area of my life, and with Your help, I now release my faith and *receive* my miracle!

Sixth Revelation:
Revelation of the Spoken Word

The words I speak have the power to change my circumstances and others for better or worse. There is life and death in my tongue!

Chapter Review!

1. I will speak *words of faith* until I receive my miracle.
2. I believe my miracle is in *my mouth* as I speak the Word of God.
3. I will be careful not to speak negative words that bring death—but rather speak words of life as I *believe and receive* God's faithful provision.

Whosoever shall say unto this mountain, Be thou removed, and be thou cast into the sea; and shall not doubt in his heart, but shall believe that those things which he saith shall come to pass; he shall have whatsoever he saith.

Mark 11:23-24

Stop! Meditate once again on the entire chapter before going on!

In the next chapter, we will discuss some things that can hinder receiving your miracle. Often when these things are removed, miracles happen!

Chapter 7

Hindrances to Your Miracle

Would not God search this out?
For he knows the secrets of the heart.

Psalms 44:21

We know that in healing deliverance ministry, there are things that can hinder us from receiving a miracle. We've seen that often when these things are dealt with, miracles happen. When the *revelation of the truth* is understood, embraced, and acted upon, what seems impossible becomes a reality.

What are some of the most prevalent *hindrances* affecting people's lives today? Please note this list is not exhaustive, as there may be others affecting your personal life that are not discussed. However, it is important that you *name, renounce,* and *forsake* each area, in order to receive the release you need for your miracle. Keeping this in mind, let's now look a little deeper, as we begin to examine our hearts.

Often when hindrances are renounced, miracles manifest!

1. Unconfessed Sin: Lack of Repentance

Confess your faults one to another, and pray one for another, that ye may be healed. The effectual fervent prayer of a righteous man availeth much.

James 5:16

If I regard iniquity in my heart, the Lord will not hear me.

Psalms 66:18

(pride, anger, bitterness, resentment, unfaithfulness, disobedience, rebellion, sexual immorality, etc.)

Sin no more, lest a worse thing come upon you.

John 5:14

2. Doubt and Unbelief:

Whatsoever is not of faith is sin.

Romans 14:23

And he (Jesus) could there do no mighty work, save that he laid his hands upon a few sick folk, and healed them. And he marveled because of their unbelief.

Mark 6:5–6

3. Unforgiveness:

For if ye forgive men their trespasses, your heavenly Father will also forgive you.

Matthew 6:14

4. Occult Involvement:

There shall not be found among you anyone who makes his son or his daughter pass through the fire, or one who practices witchcraft, or a soothsayer, or one who interprets omens, or a sorcerer, or one who conjures spells, or a medium, or a spiritist, or one who calls up the dead. For all who do these things are an abomination to the Lord.

Deuteronomy 18:10–12

(fortune telling, astrology, tarot cards, automatic writing, charms, horoscopes, Ouija boards, hypnotism, palm reading, séances, spiritism, etc.)

5. Demonic Oppression or Bondage:

Behold, there was a woman which had a spirit of infirmity eighteen years, and was bowed together, and could in no wise lift up herself. But when Jesus saw her, He called her to Him and said to her, "Woman, you are loosed from your infirmity." And He laid His hands on her, and immediately she was made straight, and glorified God." Jesus said, "Ought not this woman, being a daughter of Abraham, whom Satan hath bound these eighteen years, be loosed?"

Luke 13:16

6. Generational Curses:

Visiting the iniquity of the fathers upon the children to the third and fourth generations...

Exodus 20:5

7. Fear:

There is no fear in love; but perfect love casteth out fear: because fear hath torment. He that feareth is not made perfect in love.

1 John 4:18

8. Disappointment:

A certain woman, which had an issue of blood twelve years, and had suffered many things of many physicians, and had spent all that she had, and was nothing bettered, but rather grew worse.

Mark 5:26

9. People

And many charged him (blind Bartimaeus) that he should hold his peace: but he cried the more a great deal, Thou Son of David, have mercy on me.

Mark 10:48

10. Unbiblical Teaching:

Jesus speaking to religious leaders: You make the Word of God of no effect through Your tradition which you have handed down.

Mark 7:13

11. Failure of Leaders to Pray the Prayer of Faith:

Is any sick among you? Let him call for the elders of the church; and let them pray over him, anointing him with oil in the name of the Lord: And the prayer of faith shall save the sick, and the Lord shall raise him up; and if he have committed sins, they shall be forgiven him. Confess your faults one to another, and pray one for another, that ye may be healed. The effectual fervent prayer of a righteous man availeth much.

James 5:14—16

12. Ungodly Soul Ties:

Be ye not unequally yoked together with unbelievers: for what fellowship hath righteousness with unrighteousness? And what communion hath light with darkness?

2 Corinthians 6:14

13. Deception:

Jesus said, "Take heed that no one deceives you." For many shall come in my name, saying, I am Christ; and shall deceive many.

Matthew 24:4—5

14. Believing a Lie:

We have made a covenant with death, and with hell are we at agreement; when the overflowing scourge shall pass through, it shall not come unto us: for we have made lies our refuge, and under falsehood have we hid ourselves.

Isaiah 28:15

15. Unholy Oaths: Fraternities, Sororities, Secret Societies

Ye have heard that it hath been said by them of old time, Thou shalt not forswear thyself (take false oaths), but shalt perform unto the Lord thine oaths: But I say unto you, swear not at all; neither by heaven; for it is God's throne: Nor by the earth; for it is his footstool.

Matthew 5:33-35

Stop! Let's search our hearts, reflecting on the above!

Now that you are aware of possible hindrances, take a moment to *confess and repent* of any that may apply, as you consecrate your life of holiness and obedience to the Lord. Do take this seriously! These hindrances are real and affect our lives adversely, and because of them, many prayers have gone unanswered. I encourage you to seek out deliverance ministry as needed in order to find release and freedom in these areas. Now, let's make the following *confession of faith*, as we pray *out loud* together.

Confession of Faith

Lord Jesus, I now renounce every hindrance, as I make a decision to *turn away* from all that is sin (name each one) with a repentant heart. I believe that as I confess my sins, *"You are faithful and just to forgive me and cleanse me from all unrighteousness"* (1 John 1:9). I now declare that I no longer give place to these things in my life, and I receive Your forgiveness, in Your precious name, I pray. Amen.

Seventh Revelation:
Revelation of Hindrances

Dealing with certain hindrances or strongholds in my life through repentance can bring the manifestation of my miracle!

Chapter Review!

1. I understand that things from my past or present can keep me from receiving my miracle because they are sin.
2. I understand I must repent and turn away from everything God says is unholy.
3. I will continue to be aware of anything that could hinder me from receiving my miracle, now and in the future.

"I applied mine heart to know, to search and seek out wisdom and the reason of things..."

—Ecclesiastes 7:25

Stop! Meditate on the whole chapter as needed!

In the next chapter, we will discuss our need for *deliverance*, which can often bring the release of your miracle!

Chapter 8

The Miracle of Deliverance

*O keep my soul, and deliver me:
let me not be ashamed;
for I put my trust in thee.*

—Psalms 25:20

Anything that you struggle with is a stronghold in your life which requires deliverance!

Today, there is a tremendous need for *deliverance ministry* throughout the Church and the world. Obtaining freedom in Christ requires a total release from all forms of *demonic activity* in order to achieve wholeness in body, soul, mind, and spirit.

You may be struggling today with something that you've tried unsuccessfully to overcome—something that seems to have a *stronghold* on your life, and no matter how hard you've tried, you can't seem to gain the victory. You've tried everything you know to do to get set free, but nothing seems to help.

The *good news* is that Jesus came not only to take the penalty for our sins but to also set captives free from every form of bondage known to man—those who are bound in their mind, will, emotions, and many forms of physical illness.

What Is Deliverance?

What does it mean to be delivered or *set free?* It is being released from all torment, oppression, or anything that you may be struggling with on a regular or ongoing basis. *Oppression* is defined as *prolonged cruel* or unjust treatment or *control*. It's true that Jesus spent at least one-third of his ministry setting captives free, which he declared he was sent to do. As we look at the following scriptures, you will see that like Jesus, we have been given power over all the power of the enemy!

How God anointed Jesus of Nazareth with the Holy Ghost and with power: who went about doing good, and healing all that were oppressed of the devil; for God was with him.

—Acts 10:38

For we wrestle not against flesh and blood (people), but against principalities, against powers, against the rulers of the darkness of this world, against spiritual wickedness in high places.

—Ephesians 6:12

Wherefore take unto you the whole armor of God, that ye may be able to withstand in the evil day, and having done all, to stand.

—Ephesians 6:13

Behold, I give unto you power to tread on serpents and scorpions, and over all the power of the enemy: and nothing shall by any means hurt you.

—*Luke 10:19*

Submit yourselves therefore to God. Resist the devil, and he will flee from you.

—*James 4:7*

Stop! Take time to meditate on the above scriptures!

The deliverance process is setting many free today from all forms of bondage!

Do I Need Deliverance?

How can I know if I need deliverance? Generally, if you sincerely want to be free of something in your life, and you have sought help and still have found no relief, there most likely is a spiritual stronghold or strongholds that are keeping you in bondage.

Symptoms of Demon Oppression

Although there are many, here are some of the most common symptoms:

Fear, rejection, addictions, compulsive behaviors, lying, guilt, sudden sickness, uncontrollable anger, poverty, doubt of salvation, nightmares, abnormal sexual desire, confusion, inability to believe when you want to, rebellion, criminal activity, a sense of being driven, no peace or rest, self-hatred, self-mutilation, mental anguish, abnormal strength, inability to worship, difficulty reading the Bible and praying, jealousy, accusation, condemnation, pride, heaviness, insanity, judgmental attitudes, a critical spirit, lust, worry, depression, mental problems, prone to accidents, emotional instability, low self-esteem, harshness, rebellion, abuse, stubbornness, violence, unforgiveness, bitterness, superiority, control, manipulation, lack of submission, shame, intimidation, timidity, fear of man, inferiority, selfishness, and greed.

(See Section: "Declare Your Miracle")

Stop! Take time again for meditation. Which of the above do you struggle with on a regular basis?

My purpose in addressing this subject is to *alert you* and perhaps encourage you to consider deliverance ministry as a possible answer to your need. Also, there are a number of wonderful books that will give you much more information.

(See Section: "Recommended Reading for Further Study")

Continue to Seek the Truth

I firmly believe that we *all need* to go through the *deliverance process* and learn how to *maintain our deliverance* throughout our lifetime. This is something I do on a regular basis. We have all given Satan the *legal right* to influence our lives adversely as a result of sin. This access must be revoked in order to become completely free from all that has held us captive.

Freedom Through Deliverance

Today, I can say that I have experienced freedom from much torment and oppression that had held me captive throughout much of my life. *Generational curses* have been broken of abuse, depression, control and manipulation, rejection, and so much more. Nevertheless, remember deliverance is an *ongoing process* that we need to maintain. As long as the enemy and demonic powers are still free to harass us, we will have struggles.

Personal deliverance is an option for you that you need to consider!

But there's *good news*! Jesus said, "These things I have spoken unto you, that in me ye might have peace. In the world ye shall have tribulation: but be of good cheer; I have overcome the world." (John 16:33).

Released From Many Demons

Many come for deliverance ministry seeking relief often as a *last resort*. Tormented souls with physical, mental, and emotional problems stemming from painful experiences throughout their lifetime—and sometimes from generational curses that have been passed down through the bloodline of their ancestors. Nevertheless, many have been released from demonic spirits that have oppressed them for many years.

A woman, who was under a great deal of torment, came to me for ministry—so much so that she found difficulty in performing the simplest of tasks. She suffered with severe depression and even struggled to pray and read her Bible. She had previously served as a missionary for a number of years abroad. After several sessions, through the deliverance process, she was greatly relieved as a number of spirits were renounced and cast out.

Unfortunately, because she did not continue to come for further ministry that was needed, she was not totally set free. When I last saw her, she was still very much oppressed. Remember, we said earlier that sometimes demons that have been cast out will *return if allowed,* bringing others with them, which results in even greater bondage. This is so tragic, when we know that we can be completely delivered because of the work of the cross. Jesus has provided deliverance for all who *will receive it.*

Although, it is impossible in this short writing to share with you all that you need to know about deliverance, it is important that you understand and recognize your adversary the devil and his kingdom, who is and has been behind much heartache and loss throughout your lifetime. I pray that you will stand in faith with the *whole armor* of God and *take back what's been stolen* from you and those around you (Ephesians 6:10-18).

That old serpent, called the devil, and Satan, which deceives the whole world: he was cast out into the earth, and his angels were cast out with him. (Revelations 12:9).

Remember, when you understand the truth and receive revelation from the Holy Spirit, you can be set free. The thief will have to make *full restitution*, sevenfold!

Turn us again, O God, and cause thy face to shine; and we shall be saved.

Psalms 80:3

The thief does not come except to steal, and to kill, and to destroy. I have come that they may have life, and that they may have it more abundantly.

John 10:10

But if he (the thief) be found, he shall restore sevenfold.

Proverbs 6:31

What Can I Do Now?

First, make sure you have made the important decision to accept Jesus Christ as your Savior and Lord, repenting of all sin and surrendering your life to Him. Only as a child of God do we have the power and authority to stand against satan so we can receive God's promises. "Behold, I give you the authority to trample on serpents and scorpions, and over all the power of the enemy, and nothing shall by any means hurt you" (Luke 10:19).

Now, let's boldly declare *out loud* the following confession!

Confession of Faith

Lord Jesus, I repent of my sins and receive You as my Savior and my Lord. I invite You to come into my life right now. I want to live for You from this day forward. I look to You to save, heal, and deliver me from all torment and oppression—restoring to me everything that has been stolen and destroyed.

Devil, as a child of God, I declare that you are under my feet (2 Samuel 22:38—39), and I demand that you give back everything you have stolen from me, sevenfold. This day I come in the name of Jesus, and I demand that you restore the following things. (Name each one.)

Now, Father, as I stand in faith, I expect *full restitution* according to the heavenly settlement that You have provided for me. In the mighty name of Jesus, I pray. Amen.

(Make this your daily confession)

Eighth Revelation:
Revelation of Deliverance

Freedom from all bondage is the birthright of every *believer*. It's time I *take back all that's been stolen* from me and help others to do the same!

Chapter Review!

1. I can be *set free* from everything that holds me in bondage.
2. I must *resist* my adversary, the devil, and take back what's mine.
3. As a child of God, I have been given *power over all* the power of the enemy.
4. The *deliverance process* will bring the release I need and teach me how to remain free throughout my lifetime.

Many are the afflictions of the righteous: but the Lord delivereth him out of them all. He keepeth all his bones: not one of them is broken. Evil shall slay the wicked: and they that hate the righteous shall be desolate. The Lord redeemeth the soul of his servants: and none of them that trust in him shall be desolate.

Psalms 34: 19-22

Stop! Meditate on this chapter as needed!

Wounds in your soul can also cause great *emotional pain* throughout your lifetime. In the next chapter, let's consider how we can be set free from all torment in our mind, will, and emotions!

Chapter 9

The Miracle of Inner Healing

*The righteous cry, and the Lord heareth,
and delivereth them out of all their troubles.
The Lord is nigh unto them that are of a broken heart;
and saveth such as be of a contrite spirit.
Many are the afflictions of the righteous:
but the Lord delivereth him out of them all.*

Psalms 34:17-19

Did you ever wonder why, without warning, you can *feel emotional pain* when you think of something that happened to you a long time ago—even as far back as your childhood? Let's find out why and learn what to do about it.

During our lifetime, we have all experienced circumstances that have deeply wounded us—affecting the way we think, the decisions we make, and how we feel. These wounds are *caused by sin*, "For all have sinned, and come short of the glory of God" (Romans 3:23); and have resulted in much harm and pain. God wants to *heal every wound* in your soul. This process is called *inner healing*.

Can My Broken Heart Really Be Healed?

It is my personal testimony that I have experienced healing and wholeness in my soul as well as my physical body. There were many wounds that caused much heartache throughout my entire life. You will find that being set free from emotional torment is a process, and one that must be *maintained*. As long as you live in this world, "offences will come" (Matthew 18:7), painful circumstances will occur, and *wounds will be formed* in your soul.

You can begin the process of experiencing inner healing today!

As you read on, you will learn how to obtain the relief you need and *find peace* within. Jesus made this possible through His death on the cross. Jesus wants to heal your broken heart and bind up your wounds. Let's learn how together.

> *The Spirit of the Lord is upon me... he hath sent me to heal the brokenhearted... to set at liberty them that are bruised.*
>
> Luke 4:18–19

What is the Soul?

Created in the image of God with a body, soul, and spirit—your soul contains your mind or intellect, your will, and your emotions. Jesus had total dominion over satan and his kingdom because there *were no wounds in His soul* caused by sin (Hebrews 4:15).

Why Do I Hurt So Bad When I Think About My Past?

We know that sin gives demonic powers the *legal right* to torment and oppress us. That painful thing that happened in the past affects our decisions and causes us to feel emotional pain in our everyday lives.

When painful things happen to you, wounds are formed in your soul!

It's time that we recognize that guilt, shame, fear, depression, anger, jealousy, insecurity, and many other *troubling emotions* have as their source, a spirit that has been given the legal right to harass and torment our soul.

However, when we repent of all sin, we have the power and authority, in the name of Jesus, to bind and cast out every tormenting spirit that has *attached itself to these wounds.* When we do, we will be filled with peace and a sense of freedom as each wound is healed.

What About My Physical Body?

We also know that many *physical afflictions* have been caused as a result of the wounds in our soul. Painful thoughts and emotions over a period of time can affect our body's well-being and can cause much sickness and disease.

When we don't forgive those who have hurt us, *a lack of forgiveness* can affect our physical body as well (Matthew 6:14–15).

For example, arthritis has been found to be linked with an unforgiving heart. However, where there is repentance, physical health has been restored.

Yes, when wounds are healed in the soul, physical symptoms often go away as well! Taking every thought captive, we must *refuse to think hurtful thoughts* and resist every harmful emotion as stated in (2 Corinthians 10:5). When consistently done, we will experience a release from torment and demonic oppression. This again requires *perseverance*, for we know we have the victory in Christ, "if we faint not," as stated in (Galatians 6:9).

Often when the wounds in your soul are healed, physical well-being is restored as well!

Stop! Let's meditate on the above!

Steps to Inner Healing

Every soul wound can and must be healed. As long as there is a wound in your soul, something you *see or hear* can trigger emotional pain at any time. So how do we get our wounds healed? We must take care of the *sin that made the wound* in the first place! The following simple steps have been used by many in the process of obtaining inner healing:

1. *Repent* of the sin that caused each wound.
2. Spend time focusing on *forgiving* yourself or anyone who has caused each wound.
3. Put the *blood of Jesus* on the sin that caused each wound and invite the power of the Holy Spirit to heal each wound.

As you *wait in God's presence*, allow the Holy Spirit to touch each wound. See with your spiritual eyes, the eyes of your heart, each wound being healed. Press in through *distractions* and make the following *confession.* As you do this, you will, in time, notice that you no longer feel the pain you once did because each wound has been healed within your soul. Some wounds will take longer to heal than others due to the severity of the circumstances or trauma that caused the pain. But let no wound, no matter how small, remain. God wants you healed and set free—our souls at peace and filled with joy.

Stop! You will need to meditate on what you have just read in order to put into practice these steps and the process of inner healing!

Let me say at this point that once again, you may want to seek out those who are skilled in *deliverance ministry* to assist you during this process. I encourage you to do so, as you may find it necessary.

Many have been set free through inner healing, and you can too!

As stated previously, I believe we all need to be set free through the deliverance process, where there are areas that continue to cause us emotional pain. Many have overlooked this option, which can bring you the relief you so desperately need. *Waves of Glory Miracle Ministries* and other ministries as well are being raised up to provide healing and deliverance for you today.

Let's now make the following declaration together, *out loud*, as we begin this process of inner healing!

Confession of Faith

Father, I believe that every wound in my soul is being healed by the power of Your Holy Spirit in the light of Your presence. The sun of righteousness, Jesus Christ, is arising with "healing wings" (rays) as stated in Malachi 4:2. I decree that Your light is now shining into the deepest parts of my soul, releasing healing virtue on each and every wound. I now bind and cast out every unclean spirit that may be attached to each wound, in Jesus's name, I pray. Amen.

(Name each spirit as the Holy Spirit reveals them to you—fear, anger, rebellion, unbelief, depression, anxiety, rejection, sorrow, etc. The list found in section "Declare Your Miracle" will assist you in this process.

Remember to deal with *one wound* at a time. Again, some wounds will take longer to heal depending on the severity of each wound.

Begin to Declare

Father, I repent of the sin that caused this wound, (name it) and I forgive all who may have caused this wound in the past. (Name them.) I put the blood of Jesus on the wound, and I ask you, Holy Spirit, to release Your healing virtue as You touch this wound and bring the needed healing. Lord, I thank You now, as You begin the process of restoring my soul to perfect health. In the name of Jesus, I pray. Amen.

Resisting the Enemy

Declare every wound healed as you resist the enemy!

Once again, during this process, bind and cast out any spirit that has attached itself to each wound—that specific painful emotion you feel when remembering the circumstances at the time the wound occurred. The following statements will assist you:

1. Depression, I *bind and cast you out*, in Jesus's name.
2. Grief and despair, I *renounce you* and give you no place in my life, in Jesus's name.
3. Anger and bitterness, I *command you* to go now. I bind and cast you out, in Jesus's name.

Stop! Meditate on the above. Take as much time as you need to fully understand the process!

Inner Healing Testimony

After years of suffering and much loss, I have experienced the release of deep emotional pain and inner healing from both physical and emotional abuse, rejection, abandonment, betrayal, jealousy, manipulation and control, false accusations, and much more, which created mental and emotional wounds in my soul.

Knowing that for many, this wounding can result in physical illness as well, I am very grateful that through prayer, my relationship with the Lord, and the soothing that comes from the release of many tears, I have been spared for the most part the additional suffering that often results in some form of physical illness. I trust that my testimony will encourage you to seek your inner healing as well. It's yours as you release *expectant faith* and take *active steps* to receive your healing.

It will encourage you to know that if you will act upon the revelations discussed in this writing, you too can experience the *new birth* that we have discussed and *divine health* and *deliverance*. These truths will set you free, if you will believe and receive them and *act upon* them. As you begin to act and release your faith, miracles will become a way of life for you and those around you.

Isn't it time that we begin to live the *supernatural life* Jesus came to give us? Miracles should be a *normal* part of your everyday life!

Let me say again that I am grieved to see what satan has done to each one of us; with all too often little resistance on our part. When are we going to stop allowing the enemy to assault and destroy us one by one? Thankfully, there are more and more who are *walking in the truth*. It is my heartfelt prayer that you will too! We must stand as one, supporting one another until we can say together, *"I am totally free!"*

How Will I Know When My Soul Is Healed?

This is a very important question. As you continue the inner healing process, you will know that a wound is healed when you can *remember* that painful event and no longer feel the emotional pain you once felt. I can't begin to tell you what a difference in my life *inner healing* has made. I no longer feel the *emotional torment* that I once did. Now I can think about painful memories from the past with peace in my heart and even joy. I know that God loves me and my future is secure in His wonderful hands.

When you don't feel pain anymore your wounds are healed!

Healed of a Traumatic Childhood

Christina came from a family of 10 children and severely abusive parents. Let's listen to her story in her own words.

"My father was an alcoholic who drank away his paychecks, leaving us often without food and the necessities of life. I remember being given moldy bread to eat or nothing at all. The only food we had many times was provided by our school lunch program. We were skin and bones growing up but managed to survive our childhood years by God's grace.

When drunk, our father would beat our mother and all of us kids severely, so we lived in constant fear from the rage that was visited upon us. I remember when very little, being thrown through a window. We rarely received medical help for physical injuries. We were not taken to the doctor but were reprimanded if we did get sick, because there was no money for doctors. I remember being locked in the closet for many hours for punishment. It was so dark all I could do was cry out to God for help.

I remember one time I stepped on a rusty nail which resulted in a locked jaw and I received no medical attention. As a child I was also molested and raped on two occasions by men from the neighborhood. Abusive treatment continued into my adult years as well.

Because of these traumatic experiences, although I did accept Jesus as my Savior as a young adult, for many years I found it difficult to really allow Him to love me, as I continued to live with physical and emotional scars from the past.

"The *good news* is that through *'Waves of Glory Miracle Ministries'*, I received the help I needed through healing deliverance ministry, as I experienced 'inner healing' from the many wounds in my soul. Today I have been set free from strongholds that had kept me captive for most of my life. I am so grateful to this ministry for sharing 'The Truth' with me, so I could be set free from the torment that held me captive for many years.

Through healing prayer and the love and compassion of God's precious people, you too can experience healing and wholeness in your life. God loves you so much! As you reach out by faith, what He's done for myself and many others, He will do for you."

Breaking Harmful Soul Ties

Before closing this chapter, it's important we take a moment to discuss the effect *ungodly soul ties* can have upon our lives. If you are experiencing painful emotions as a result of a past or present relationship, most likely the soul tie in the spirit still exists and *must be broken.*

In the spirit realm, a soul tie is created when we enter into a relationship with another person. It may be a healthy relationship, which results in our well-being, or an unhealthy relationship with negative repercussions. Ungodly soul ties can have a devastating effect upon us, as painful emotions continue to torment our souls long after the relationship has ended—affecting our lives adversely—physically, mentally, emotionally, and spiritually.

Remember, your emotions are a part of your soul, along with your will and intellect or your thought-life. Ungodly soul ties can be completely broken, and our souls set free. There are *steps* we can take to break an unhealthy soul tie.

Once again, *repent* for entering into any harmful relationship apart from the will of God, which has produced sin. Then, *forgive* yourself and each person with whom you had an unhealthy relationship in the past or present. Now, make a decision to surrender your life in obedience to God, trusting Him to bring the emotional healing you need in order to have peace and wholeness restored.

Please note that some soul ties are harder to break than others because of the length of time in the relationship and the strength of the soul tie. Nevertheless, continue to *declare each soul tie broken* in the name of Jesus. In time, wounds created by ungodly relationships in your soul will be completely healed, and painful emotions will no longer bring torment.

Do pray the following prayer *out loud* until you experience relief and all emotional pain is gone. Remember, we know the wounds in our soul are healed when we no longer feel emotional pain when remembering painful memories of the past.

Prayer to Break Unhealthy Soul Ties

Many have found relief after breaking unhealthy soul ties created during past relationships!

Heavenly Father, I desire to be set free from every ungodly soul tie formed during my lifetime. I now break every soul tie and repent of all sin, forgiving myself and (name each person). I now take back what I gave to _____ and what was taken from me. I make a *decision* today to let go of every ungodly relationship, trusting You to set me free from every painful memory, and I ask You to restore what the enemy has stolen—filling every void with Your presence. I thank You for this new day of freedom. In Jesus's name, I pray. Amen.

Let Me Pray for You!

Heavenly Father, I pray that the one reading this book will experience a changed and transformed life by the power of Your Holy

Spirit. May they find the "peace that passes all understanding" (Philippians 4:6–7) in knowing Jesus as Savior, Healer, and Deliverer. I now decree and declare that their eyes be *supernaturally opened* and that they will receive the revelation necessary so that they can experience their miracle today.

Thank You, Lord, for Your touch and for releasing Your power to meet every need for Your glory. Do it now, Lord. I command every sickness to go, every loss suffered to be restored, every unacceptable situation to be turned around, and every need to be supplied in the mighty name of Jesus. Amen.

Ninth Revelation: Revelation of Inner Healing

Emotional pain is triggered in my soul because there are wounds that need to be healed by the power of the Holy Spirit!

Chapter Review

1. When painful circumstances occur in my life, wounds are created in my soul that need to be healed.
2. These wounds can cause mental, emotional, and physical illness.
3. Through repentance and perseverance, I can be completely set free.
4. Healing deliverance ministry is available to assist me in the process of inner healing from all pain and suffering.

"He heals the broken-hearted, and binds up their wounds."

Psalms 147:3

Stop! Meditate until the truth becomes revelation for you!

Finally, let's consider the *greatest miracle of all*, which is truly the greatest gift of all!

Chapter 10

The Greatest Miracle of All

And this is the record that God has given to us eternal life, and this life is in His Son.

1 John 5:11

This writing would not be complete without considering God's greatest gift to mankind—the free gift of eternal life. It has been said that this greatest of miracles is seen in the *new birth* experience, when one is *'born again'* through faith in Jesus Christ as Savior and Lord. Spiritual change occurs, "old things pass away and all things become new" (2 Corinthians 5:17).

Let's consider how you can experience salvation, the assurance that heaven is your home, and that your name has been written in "The Lamb's Book of Life" (Revelation 21:27).

For God so loved the world, that He gave His only begotten Son, that whosoever believeth in Him should not perish, but have everlasting life. For God sent not His Son into the world to condemn the world; but that the world through Him might be saved. He that believeth on Him is not condemned: but he that believeth not is condemned already, because he hath not believed in the name of the only begotten Son of God.

John 3:16-18

What Must I Do to Be Saved?

Step One: One Must Believe

God's Son willingly left heaven and came to earth to save every man, woman, and child from eternal destruction and separation from God. The Word of God says, "Neither is there salvation in any other: for there is none other name under heaven given among men, whereby we must be saved" (Acts 4:12).

Apostle Paul wrote,

"For I am not ashamed of the gospel of Christ: for it is the power of God unto salvation to everyone that believeth."

Romans 1:16

Step Two: One Must Confess

For with the heart man believeth unto righteousness; and with the mouth confession is made unto salvation.

Romans 10:10

Step Three: One Must Receive

But as many as received him, to them gave he power to become the sons of God, even to them that believe on his name.

John 1:12

So we see, *Jesus did it all* for us. All we have to do is *believe*. We don't have to work for this free gift of salvation as many people think, but just believe in what Jesus did on the cross. When He died and suffered there, He provided a way for everyone to come back to God. *No longer separated*, we can walk and talk with Him here on earth. We can have His peace, love, joy, and His help and protection right here, right now!

There are some who believe that Jesus is the Son of God and may have even said a prayer for salvation at one time, but their lives have not changed. They have not allowed God to *be in control* of their lives. They have not welcomed Jesus into their hearts. When people have truly given their lives to Jesus Christ and have been *reborn by God's spirit, real change* will be evident. "By their fruits ye shall know them" (Matthew 7:20).

Now, having heard the Word of God, we see that each of us must make the most important decision of our lives: to *believe and receive or reject God's free gift* of eternal life. If you have not accepted the Savior, God the Father has given to us, I would like to invite you to do so at this time.

Before you make your decision, please know that the many promises of God found in the Scriptures are only for those who have put their faith in God's Son. With Christ in our hearts and lives, we can now claim all that is ours through Him—the forgiveness of our sins, divine health, healing, deliverance, prosperity, and every provision for life.

Stop! There's much here to meditate on. This is indeed the most important decision you will ever make in your lifetime!

Now, with a heart full of faith, let's make the following confession together *out loud!*

Confession of Faith

Lord Jesus, come into my life. I repent of my sin and believe and receive You as my Savior and Lord. I give You complete control of my heart and life. I believe that You are the one and only Son of God who gave Your life for me on the cross of Calvary so I could have *eternal life* in heaven. I dedicate and commit my life to You, and I now, by faith, receive all that You have provided for me. I ask You to baptize me with Your Holy Spirit and with fire that I may be mightily used by You for Your glory. I want to be a vessel of honor—reaching out to others who are hurting and in need of Your salvation and healing power. I want to tell the whole world what You have done for me. Thank You, Lord Jesus. Amen.

Tenth Revelation:
Revelation of Triune Salvation

The gift of salvation purchased by Jesus Christ on the cross of Calvary is threefold: forgiveness of my sins, provision of divine health for my body, soul, mind, and spirit, and deliverance from every form of bondage!

Chapter Review!

1. I can be saved, healed, and delivered through faith in Jesus Christ.
2. According to the Word of God, I must *believe, confess, and receive* God's gift of salvation by faith in the Son of God who died in my place on Calvary's cross.
3. As a child of God, all of God's promises and blessings are mine to receive by faith.

"He that hath the Son hath life; and he that hath not the Son of God hath not life. These things have I written unto you that believe on the name of the Son of God; that you may know that you have Eternal Life, and that you may believe on the name of the Son of God. And this is the confidence that we have in Him, that if we ask anything according to His will, He hears us: And if we know that He hears us, whatsoever we ask, we know that we have the petitions that we desired of Him."

1 John 5:12-15

Stop! Meditate as needed once more!

"Let the truth be told! Shout it from the rooftops!"

Epilogue

*The things which are impossible with
men are possible with God.*

Luke 18:27

In 2011, I received this word from the Lord in an inner audible voice: *"Let the truth be told! Shout it from the rooftops!"* This word has compelled me with compassion of heart to proclaim *the truth* of the gospel of Jesus Christ—the provision of the forgiveness of sins, divine health, and deliverance from all that holds us captive. Therefore, throughout this writing, I have emphasized the fact that *the truth* must be revisited many times before that truth becomes heart-felt and life-changing.

In 1685, Jeanne Guyon, in her classic writing *Experiencing the Depths of Jesus Christ: The Autobiography*, wrote, "The Lord's chief desire is to reveal Himself to you... There are mysteries hidden in the 'revelation of God,' and to enjoy them fully is to let them be imprinted deeply in your spirit." May the Lord give you the understanding that you must have and supernaturally enlighten you as you press on toward a lifestyle of miracles.

I trust that you will no longer accept symptoms of sickness or anything that tries to bring loss, torment, or destruction to your life because you now *know the truth*—and that you will resist the devil with every fiber of your being as a child of God—standing upon God's Word and the authority He has given you as you take back what's been stolen.

We have said that all too often, those who seek a miracle are *waiting for God to do what He's already done* as they look to another person or ministry for their miracle. The truth is, *you can and must* learn to *release your faith*, and you must *choose* to *receive* your miracle as you act upon the revelations that God has given in His Word.

Then, let's not stop there but *continue* to live a life of expectation that receives whatever you need each and every day. This is what Jesus meant when He said, "The thief cometh not, but for to steal, and to kill, and to destroy: I am come that they might have life, and that they might have it more abundantly" (John 10:10).

Again, let me say that receiving your miracle is really *up to you*. We know it is God's will to save, heal, and deliver us and that every provision has already been made. Nevertheless, it's up to you to *believe and receive* God's best and never settle for less.

Our discussion would not be complete without considering the sovereignty of God with regard to healing and deliverance ministry. When all is said and done, *Jesus is Lord*, and He can do whatever He chooses to do in a person's life or situation. This we must always keep in mind. Yes, we must do all we can to obey God's Word, take action where and whenever possible, and always *leave the results* with Him!

Now, before we close, let's take a moment to review the *ten revelations* we've discussed together:

1. I must *know the truth* by divine revelation from the Word of God!
2. I must *believe and expect* my miracle today!
3. I must *walk by faith* with a heart full of expectation!
4. I must make a decision to *receive* my miracle!

5. I must actively *resist* any attempt of the enemy to steal my miracle!
6. I must *choose* to speak words of life and not death!
7. I must *renounce* anything in my life that would hinder me from receiving my miracle!
8. I must *seek deliverance* daily and live free from all torment and oppression!
9. I must seek and *expect* the Holy Spirit to heal the wounds in my soul!
10. I must *embrace salvation's free gift* of forgiveness of sins, divine healing and health, and deliverance from all.

Let's Pray!

Heavenly Father, I thank You for those who are seeking a miracle today. I thank You for the faith You have given each one so that they can believe and receive their miracle. Thank You for Your willingness and desire to hear the cry of every heart and for giving each one ears to hear and eyes to see and understand by revelation *the truths* of Your Word.

To each of you who have diligently persevered through the pages of this book, I pray that the supernatural power of God will touch you now. I declare that divine health and healing are yours and that miracles manifest in your life this very day—every form of bondage broken, freedom from all torment, oppression, and unacceptable circumstances.

I release over you now the Lord's abundant provision in every area of your life, and I bind any work of the enemy that would try to steal and destroy that which is yours by *inheritance* as a child of God.

May the peace of God be with you in the fullness of the Holy Spirit as He fills you with His love and assurance that truly with God all things are possible to those who *believe* (Mark 9:23). In the wonderful name of Jesus, I pray. Amen.

Do write to me and let me know what God has done for you so that we may rejoice together in His goodness. God bless you!

(See Section: "About the Author")

Pastor Mary Ellen Gordon
Waves of Glory Miracle Ministries
1610 Old Manor Drive, Derby, NY 14047

Email: wavesofgloryministry@gmail.com
Website: *www.wavesofglorymiracleministry.wordpress.com*

The following section will be of great help to you as you use the *authority* God has given you as a believer to declare your miracle!

Declare Your Miracle

Evening, and morning, and at noon, will I pray, and cry aloud: and he shall hear my voice.

Psalms 55:17

Thou shalt also decree a thing, and it shall be established unto thee.

Job 22:28

Declaring your miracle is important as you *maintain your confession* of faith daily. Even though your body may be suffering with symptoms of illness or impossible circumstances continue to oppress you, God's Word is true and powerful—making that which seems impossible, possible for you today!

What you will find in this section must be *activated* and is *crucial* to your total well-being, if you are to receive all that the Lord has for you. If you will *act now*, applying what you have learned with perseverance, you can receive all that you need and desire.

Know that as you make the following daily declaration *out loud*, the Lord hears you, and every word shall be established for you. Speak with *boldness*, and release your faith until your miracle manifests! Again, if you will touch Jesus with *expectant faith*, He will meet your need today!

Daily Declaration!

Lord Jesus, I declare that You are my Savior, Healer, Deliverer, and Provider. I believe and receive my miracle today. With expectant faith, I *renounce all doubt and unbelief*. I now choose to live for You according to Your Word from this day forward. I believe Your Word *is the truth*, and I embrace the revelations You have revealed to me through Your Word. I consecrate and surrender all that I am and have to You, asking You to take my life and use it for Your glory. I believe that You are fulfilling Your plan and purpose for my life as I cooperate with You to fulfill my destiny.

With a *repentant heart*, I choose to forgive myself and everyone who has ever hurt me, and I renounce every hindrance or obstacle that would try to keep me from receiving my *full inheritance* in Jesus Christ my Lord. I ask for Your forgiveness from all sin, and I now *resist and renounce* satan and all his works. I declare that he and his kingdom have *no place in my life*, and I take back everything he has stolen and destroyed from me. I now demand and receive *sevenfold justice, restitution, and full restoration* of every loss suffered, and I resist and renounce any attempt of the enemy to hinder or steal my miracle.

I renounce every destructive circumstance, painful emotion, diagnosis, or symptom of illness, and I declare I have perfect health, wholeness, and soundness in my body, soul, mind, and spirit because of Your sacrifice for me on the cross. I now bind and cast out all *torment and oppression*, and I declare myself free from every form of bondage.

(I renounce, bind, and cast out ____, In Jesus's Name.)
(Name each spirit as it may apply to you)

(Fear, unbelief, anxiety, torment, worry, anger, grief, confusion, poverty, etc.)

(See List of Demonic Spirits)

Thank You, Lord, for divine health and deliverance and for Your faithfulness in supplying all my needs. I will continue to speak words of faith over my life and others—words of life and not death, health and not sickness, blessings and not curses, and I declare every wound in my soul healed for Your glory! I believe that You have done everything necessary so that I can now live the abundant life You have given me. I will now act upon the revelations You have revealed to me and put them into practice with Your grace and strength in Your precious name, I pray. Amen.

I Decree and Declare!

(Finish each statement with *In Jesus's Name*, using the list below as needed.)
Remember, there is power in the name of Jesus!

I believe and receive everything I need today, In Jesus's name.

I believe God is intervening in my situation right now, In Jesus's name.

I renounce all doubt, unbelief, and confusion, In Jesus's name.

I believe and receive my miracle with expectant faith, In Jesus's name.

I repent of sin and renounce every hindrance to my miracle, In Jesus's name.

I renounce and repent of (name each sin), In Jesus's name.

I forgive _____(person) for _____(offence), In Jesus's name.

I take captive every thought to the obedience of Jesus Christ, In His precious name, Amen.

For Healing!

I believe I receive my miracle today, In Jesus's name.

I believe I receive my healing from (name) In Jesus's name.

I break the power of every symptom of sickness (name each one) and command it to go from my body and soul right now, In Jesus's name.

I declare myself healed and I keep my healing, In Jesus's name.

I thank You, Lord, for providing perfect health for me, and I declare that divine health is mine today, In Jesus's name.

I renounce every diagnosis, symptom, and circumstance that would try to bring harm to myself or those around me, In Jesus's name.

For Deliverance!

I declare that I am free from all bondage, and the enemy no longer has a foothold in my life, In Jesus's name.

I believe I receive my deliverance from _____, In Jesus's name.

I resist Satan and bind and cast out _____. In Jesus's name.

(See List Below.)

I break the power of the generational curse of _____. It stops here and now, In Jesus's name.

(See List of Curses Below)

I cut the unholy soul tie with _____ (name each person) and I take back what I gave to_____ and what was taken from me, In Jesus's name.

I renounce and cast out any spirit that came to me when I _____, In Jesus's name.

I command every hindrance or obstacle be removed from my life, and I declare I am free to fulfill my destiny, In Jesus's name.

I declare that I now resist the devil and take back everything that he has stolen and destroyed in my life, In Jesus's name.

I declare that Jesus is my Savior, Healer and Deliverer, In Jesus's name.

I declare that I have perfect health, every provision and I am free from all bondage through Jesus Christ, In His precious name.

I declare I am prospering in every area of my life, In Jesus's name. (divine health, family, finances, ministry etc.)

I declare I have favor with God and man, In Jesus's name.

List of Demonic Spirits!

Please note that the list below is not all inclusive but rather consists of some of the most common spirits that can affect our lives adversely on a daily basis. Additional lists can be obtained from other deliverance ministry resources that are available.

(See Section: "Recommended Reading")

I trust that the following list will be of help to you, as you experience a release from a number of unclean spirits that seek to bring torment and oppression into your life. The good news is that we can be set free from everything that holds us captive!

- Pride
- Perfection
- Insecurity
- Fear
- Inadequacy
- Hindering Spirits
- Greed
- Accusation
- Competition
- Mockery
- Stubbornness
- Self-righteousness
- Gossip
- Sarcastic Spirit
- Critical Spirit
- Mental Illness
- Insanity
- Seizures/Epilepsy
- Double Mindedness
- Multi-personality
- Hyperactivity
- Self-mutilation
- Inferiority Complex
- Timidity
- Intimidation
- Worry
- Sensitivity
- Fear of Authority
- Nightmares
- Panic Attacks
- Phobias (dark, heights, future)
- Anxiety
- Nervousness
- Abandonment
- Procrastination
- Gloominess/Sadness
- Rejection
- Despair/Grief
- Delusion/Hearing Voices
- Fatigue
- Withdrawal
- Mind-binding
- Sleepiness
- Forgetfulness
- Stupidity
- Daydreaming
- Trances
- Laziness

Lethargy
Sluggishness/Confusion
Occult
Magic (white or black)
Spirit Guides
Inherited Curses
Guilt/Shame
Self-pity
Loneliness
Depression/Manic Depression
Suicide
Insomnia
Impatience
Bitterness
Strife
Covetousness
Gluttony
Obesity
Addiction
Anorexia
Bulimia
Infirmity
Asthma
Hay Fever
Allergies
Fever
Cancer
Death
Disease
Pain
Deception/Lies
Exaggeration
Profanity
Hypocrisy
Condemnation
Isolation
Vanity
Seducing Spirits
Prostitution

Cults
Religious Spirits
Legalism
Tradition
Control (Jezebel Spirit)
Idolatry
Revenge/Retaliation
Emotional Wrath
Suspicion
Weakness
Fornication
Adultery
Anger
Rage
Hatred
Witch, Warlock, Satanist
Murder/Abortion
Indian Curses
Santeria Curses
Roots Curses
Voo Doo Curses
Word Curses
Violence/Restlessness
Selfishness
Doubt/Unbelief
Rebellion/Witchcraft
Self-Exaltation
Sensuous Thoughts
Word Twisting
Exhibitionism
Pornography
Lust
Lesbianism
Homosexuality
Masturbation
Sodom
Bestiality
Child Molestation
Incest

Most Common Generational Curses!

The following includes some known curses that have affected many lives. A more comprehensive list can be found in some deliverance materials that are available.

(See Section: "Recommended Reading")

Alcoholism, drugs, nicotine, addictions, incest, divorce, homosexuality, abortion, sexual immorality, various sicknesses, diseases, child molestation, physical and emotional abuse, pornography, greed, murder, violence, imprisonment, fornication, adultery, divorce, control (jezebel spirit), occult, rebellion, obesity, deaths (accidents), insanity, mental illness, suicide, depression, phobias, etc.

If the Son therefore shall make you free, you shall be free indeed.

John 8:36

Prayers that Avail Much

Confess your faults one to another, and pray one for another, that ye may be healed. The effectual fervent prayer of a righteous man availeth much.

James 5:16

For the eyes of the Lord are over the righteous, and his ears are open unto their prayers: but the face of the Lord is against them that do evil.

I Peter 3:12

Remember, to those who have placed their faith in Jesus Christ as Savior and Lord, power and authority is given in Jesus's name over all the power of the enemy, as stated in (Luke 10:19). Only then will these prayers be effective so that you can receive all that is yours in Christ. (If you have not already done so, Chapter 10 will guide you in making this important decision.)

As you declare the following prayers *out loud* with a heart full of *expectant faith*, I am believing with you for every need and desire of your heart to be manifested according to *God's will*. Remember to seek out healing deliverance ministry to assist you as needed—as you *persevere and believe* that your miracle is on the way.

The lists found in the previous section, "Declare Your Miracle," will help you as you pray the following prayers.

Prayer of Repentance

Lord Jesus, I am sorry for all my sins, and I now repent, as I make a decision to turn away and no longer practice sin. I ask for Your forgiveness for _____ (Name each sin). I also repent of everything that I have or have not said or done to keep me from learning the truth. I now choose to seek Your Word and obey it. I thank You for forgiving me. In Your precious name, I pray. Amen.

Prayer for Unbelief

Holy Spirit, I choose to believe Your Word and Your promises. Forgive me for allowing doubt and unbelief to enter my life. Right now, I renounce the spirit of unbelief, and I command this spirit to leave. In the name of Jesus, I pray. Amen.

Prayer of Forgiveness

Dear Jesus, forgive me for failing to forgive those who have hurt me. Holy Spirit, show me where I have held unforgiveness in my heart and give me the grace to forgive. I now renounce all bitterness and resentment, and I make a decision to forgive myself and everyone who has caused me pain. (Name each person and what they did.) I forgive them the same way You have forgiven me, and with heartfelt faith, I receive Your forgiveness. I renounce the spirit of unforgiveness, and I bind and cast it out of my life. In Your name, I pray. Amen.

Prayer for Healing

Lord Jesus, I believe what Your Word says about healing. In Your suffering, you paid for my sickness, and by Your wounds I am healed. With all my heart, I repent for letting satan come into my life and bring sickness. I ask You to forgive me now. I am trusting in the work of the cross, and I declare myself healed. Today, I choose life. I renounce every spirit of infirmity and every spirit of pain, and I order every demonic spirit of sickness and disease to leave right now. (Name them.) I declare myself totally free in my body, mind, emotions, and spirit, and I thank You, Lord, for perfect health. In Your name, I pray. Amen.

Now, by faith take action as the Holy Spirit may direct and begin to do what you could not do physically before or as applicable to your specific situation.

Remember, as you take some kind of action, you will be releasing your faith in order to receive your miracle!

Prayer for Deliverance

Dear Jesus, I renounce every stronghold of the enemy, and I bind and cast out every spirit that came to me as a result of sin. I command them to go now and never return. (Name each one using the list)

(See Section: "Declare Your Miracle")

Thank You for setting me free. In Your name, I pray. Amen.

Prayer to Break Generational Curses

In the name of Jesus, I assume responsibility for the sins of my ancestors, and I renounce every curse inherited through our bloodline. (Name each curse. See Section: "Declare Your Miracle") Today, I loose myself from every generational curse, and I declare myself and my family free from their effects. I command every demonic spirit to leave that brought the curse in the first place, and I break your power over me and my family. I thank You, Lord Jesus, for setting me free. Amen.

Prayer for Breaking Ungodly Soul Ties

In the name of Jesus, I renounce and sever every ungodly spiritual soul tie with _____ (name each person) and I now take back what I gave to _____ and what was taken from me. Amen.

Prayer When Facing Difficult Circumstances

If you need a change in your circumstances, a breakthrough of some kind, God's favor, or restoration of that which has been destroyed or lost—ask the Holy Spirit to guide you to know what action to take in your specific situation.

Holy Spirit, I need Your help! I ask for Your wisdom to know what to do in this situation. You said to cast all my cares on You and to trust You to do what I cannot do. With the authority You have given me in Christ, I now break every assignment of the enemy against me in Jesus's name, and I thank You for showing me what action to take. Lord, I believe that You are at work in my circumstances, and I thank You for taking care of all my needs as You promised. Your will be done! I believe and receive my miracle today. In the name of Jesus, I pray. Amen.

Recommended Reading for Further Study

Healing and Divine Health

Healing the Sick by T.L. Osborn

Christ the Healer by F.F. Bosworth

Healing the Whole Man by Joan Hunter

The Lord for the Body by A.B. Simpson

You Can Be Healed by Billy Joe Daugherty

Healing by Smith Wigglesworth

Power to Heal by Joan Hunter

Jesus Heals Your Sickness Today by Guillermo Maldonado

How to Pray for Healing by Che Ahn

Daughter of Destiny by Kathryn Kuhlman

How to Heal the Sick by Charles & Francis Hunter

Healed of Cancer by Dodie Osteen

How to Live and Not Die by Norvel Hayes

Deliverance and Inner Healing

Blessing or Curse by Derek Prince

Breaking of Curses by Frank & Ida Mae Hammond

Breaking Unhealthy Soul-ties by Bill and Sue Banks

Deliverance from Evil Spirits by Francis MacNutt

Exposing and Expelling Strongholds by Paul and Claire Hollis

Expelling Demons by Derek Prince

Inner Healing and Deliverance by Apostle G. Maldonado

Pigs in the Parlor by Frank and Ida Mae Hammond

Prayers That Heal the Heart by Mark and Patti Virkler

Stolen Property Returned by John Avanzini

Unbound: A Practical Guide to Deliverance by Neal Lozano

When Pigs Move In by Don Dickerman

Demons and Deliverance by Frank & Ida Mae Hammond

Deliverance From Eating Disorders by Bill Banks

Bibliography

Avanzini, John. *Stolen Property Returned.* Tulsa, Oklahoma: Harrison House. 1984.

Guyon, Jeanne. *Experiencing the Depths of Jesus Christ.* Auburn, Maine: Seedsowers Publishing House. 1975.

Hollis, Paul and Claire. *Exposing and Expelling Strongholds.* Tampa, Florida: Warfare Publications. 2000.

Maldonado, Apostle G. *Inner Healing and Deliverance.* Miami, Florida: ERJ Publications. 2006.

Maldonado, Guillermo. *Jesus Heals Your Sickness, Today.* Miami, Florida: ERJ Publications. 2009.

Maldonado, Guillermo. *How to Walk in the Supernatural Power of God.* New Kensington, Pennsylvania: Whitaker House. 2011.

The Holy Bible, King James Version

PC Study Bible Version 5 by Biblesoft, 2007

Wilkinson, Bruce. *The Prayer of Jabez.* Sisters, Oregon: Multnomah Publishers, Inc. 2001.

About the Author

Mary Ellen Gordon is the founder and president of *Waves of Glory Miracle Ministries* located along beautiful Lake Erie in Western New York. She has been ordained a minister of the Gospel of Jesus Christ through Full Gospel Assemblies International, Parksburg, Pennsylvania, USA.

Pastor Gordon is passionate about spreading the Full Gospel of Jesus Christ here and around the world, as she teaches the Body of Christ to live victoriously by applying needed *revelations* from the Word of God.

The call to be a part of the healing ministry was given many years ago, when she experienced the *new birth* through faith in Jesus Christ in 1975. The Lord spoke at that time, "Lay hands on the sick and they will recover." At that time, the only person known to Pastor Gordon who performed miracles was the Lord Jesus Christ, as seen in the Gospels. However, later, she discovered in the Word of God, that "The Great Commission" (Mark 16:14—18) calls every believer in Christ to actively take part in bringing healing and deliverance to all in need.

Seven years later in 1981, when she received "The Baptism of the Holy Spirit," the Lord spoke again, placing within her heart, great compassion to see the lame walk, the blind see, and those sick in body, soul, and spirit *set free* for the glory of God.

Today, at God's appointed time, *Waves of Glory Miracle Ministries* has been raised up by God with the mandate of bringing the message of salvation, healing, and deliverance to the church and beyond. It's time that "The truth be told and shouted from the rooftops," words God spoke to Pastor Gordon in 2011 during an extended period of prayer and fasting.

The cry of Father's heart is "My people are perishing for a lack of knowledge" (Hosea 4:6). Tragically, too many do not know or believe that every provision for divine health, healing, and deliverance has already been made and is available today to those who will respond in faith—and receive all that has been purchased on the cross of Calvary by our Lord Jesus Christ.

Through healing seminars, conferences, miracle services, radio ministry, and a healing prayer center, now located in Western New York, Pastor Gordon seeks to fulfill the vision God has given. She is available for ministry upon request by contacting:

Waves of Glory Miracle Ministries

1610 Old Manor Dr. Derby, NY 14047
Email: *wavesdgloryministry@gmail.com*
Website: *www.wavesofglorymiracleministry.wordpress.com*

Write the vision, and make it plain upon tablets, that he may run that readeth it. For the vision is yet for an appointed time, but at the end it shall speak, and not lie: though it tarry, wait for it; because it will surely come, it will not tarry.

Habakkuk 2:2-3

"Let the Truth Be Told! Shout It from the Rooftops!"